POPE FRANCIS
AND HIS CRITICS

POPE FRANCIS

AND HIS CRITICS

Historical and
Theological Perspectives

James J. Bacik

Foreword by Martin Marty

Paulist Press
New York / Mahwah, NJ

Cover image by Alessandro Bianchi / REUTERS
Cover and book design by Sharyn Banks

Library of Congress Cataloging-in-Publication Data

Names: Bacik, James J., 1936– author.
Title: Pope Francis and his critics : historical and theological perspectives / James J. Bacik.
Description: New York : Paulist Press, [2020]
Identifiers: LCCN 2019005031 (print) | LCCN 2019011229 (ebook) | ISBN 9781587688454 (ebook) | ISBN 9780809154531 (pbk. : alk. paper)
Subjects: LCSH: Francis, Pope, 1936– —Political and social views. | Francis, Pope, 1936– —Public opinion.
Classification: LCC BX1378.7 (ebook) | LCC BX1378.7 .B33 2020 (print) | DDC 282.092—dc23
LC record available at https://lccn.loc.gov/2019005031

ISBN 978-0-8091-5453-1 (paperback)
ISBN 978-1-58768-845-4 (e-book)

Published by Paulist Press
997 Macarthur Boulevard
Mahwah, New Jersey 07430
www.paulistpress.com

Printed and bound in the United States of America

For Phillip L. Safford
my highly respected brother-in-law, a loving marriage partner
for my sister, and a dedicated father to his children,
who, guided by a steady Christian moral compass,
is generous with his time helping those with various needs,
loves nature and cares for the environment, and
lives everyday life as a witness to the power of the
Gracious Mystery

CONTENTS

FOREWORD

This small book offers giant promises. Think of it as a mini-dictionary or a mini-mini-encyclopedia that deals with topics usually addressed in multivolume formats. Yet it does not fail to deliver on its implied promise: to provide introductory comment on issues that concern Catholics (and their scholarly relatives) in the twenty-first century. Father Bacik, who shows up weekly on my web-index as "Jim Bacik," has won the respect of so many of us because of the scope, timeliness, and informational value of his entries and literary offerings.

How, one might fairly ask, can and does one reach as far and as deeply as he does here, without providing anything more than surface-skimming treatments of what it takes authors and editors of dictionaries and encyclopedias many pages to treat? Note, first, that Father Bacik is not pretending or expecting to deliver a "last word" on themes that, taken together, result in libraries full of opinions. Note, second, that he has a gift or the discipline to come to the point almost at once on each of his subjects.

How does he do this? As one who has read him for years, I'd quickly respond, How? By practice and rich experience. As a historian, I know how complicated topics such as these are. One does not gain the experience to sort out what is significant from what is ordinary on the basis of only casual experience. The author is at his task weekly (as I first came to know him through his regular commentary on biblical texts) and perennially, in the many articles and books he has written. I have seen him in action, if more briefly than I'd like, in his pastoral and priestly roles, where he addresses college or university students and faculties without apology, and nonacademic members of and worshipers at what many would call ordinary parishes. Let me insert: he treats them all as *extra*ordinary.

To bring focus to what could have been a sprawling essay on modern Catholicism, its achievements, and, especially, its current discontents, Father Bacik has wisely chosen to relate all his topics to the pontificate and person of Pope Francis, the subject of curiosity by those who occupy back pews or who are preoccupied with front pages of media coverage. I started "covering" the Church during the Second Vatican Council, which kept scholars, reporters, and Church leaders busy most waking hours for several months in four autumns. At that time, we thought that the aggiornamento promoted by Pope John XXIII and his colleagues was almost beyond imagination. In retrospect, thanks to a world and Church in turmoil, that Council looks almost petite and quiet.

Not now. Due to the nature and growth of media and the competing interests of friends and foes of the Church, there seem to be few limits to the urgencies that demand attention and inspire controversial assessments. Many of the media treatments are so obviously representations of partisan interests and prejudices that it is hard to find a course through which to navigate their demands. Father Bacik would not respect me if I suggested here that he has promised or found a way to comprehend all those interests, or to force the distance on the topics in such a way as to have enabled a sure and steady "nonpartisan" approach.

That having been said, it should become obvious to most readers that this author is not running for office, seeking preferments, or yearning for congenial company or cheap affirmations, thus skewing his attempts to be of service to the Church. We live in a time when prejudices and polarities color so much of

Foreword

Church life (or political or any other kind of life) that no one can step onto the scene and expect to be seen as "objective," "neutral," or "noncommittal." What matters now is that on such a controversial scene, the analysts, reporters, and commentators will demonstrably seek to display wisdom, learning, empathy, and in the present kind of case, love for the Church and its people with their various gifts and yearnings. Father Bacik demonstrates these generously.

On these pages, the reader meets or re-meets many of the figures who have helped set the terms for debate and action. None of them is the first person ever to write personally without risk, to observe without having opinions, or, in short, to avoid being wishy-washy. Wishy-washiness is the great weakener of commitment, the diminishing agent of spiritual and intellectual activity. As I read the clarifications offered on these pages, I figuratively raise my hand and offer, "I second the motions," and await lively, fair-minded, and worthy discussion. There is much precedent for such in biblical and later Christian study and debate, and to more of such excellence, this book and its author strike me as being dedicated and patient. I am confident that readers will find it so.

Happy the parish, classroom, or forum where Bacik-prompted framings of issues and aspirations, such as those that are so visible and exciting in this book, will prevail.

Martin E. Marty
Emeritus professor, The University of Chicago
and member of St. Luke Lutheran Church

INTRODUCTION

On March 13, 2013, a relatively unknown Jesuit cardinal, Jorge Bergoglio, the archbishop of Buenos Aires, Argentina, made a striking entrance on the world stage. Having chosen the name Francis after the great saint from Assisi, the newly elected pope stepped out onto the balcony of St. Peter's Basilica, dressed simply in the white papal cassock without the ermine cape worn by previous popes for their initial public appearance. Before giving the traditional papal blessing, Francis broke precedent by asking the crowd to do him a favor: "I ask you to pray to the Lord to bless me." The pope then bowed his head as the vast throng grew silent, an iconic moment that provides a key for interpreting his humble ministry as Bishop of Rome.

During his first five years as pope, Francis visited some thirty countries and drew large crowds, as many as 3.5 million for a Mass in Brazil. On his pastoral visit to the United States, he became the first pope to address a joint session of Congress. His innovative initiatives included appointing a Council of Cardinals to advise him on leading a global Church of 1.2 billion members. His writings, especially on human love and the environment, have generated significant discussion both within and outside the Church. On the international scene, he helped restore diplomatic relations between the United States and Cuba and promoted the Paris Agreement on climate change. He has met personally with countless persons in need, including prisoners, refugees, immigrants, the disabled, and others on the margins. He participated in the annual World Youth Days, and he presided over two synods on the family and another on youth. He has appointed about half of the 120 cardinals eligible to elect the next pope, including at least 15 from countries never represented before.

Care for the environment is now a part of Catholic social teaching due to his encyclical *Laudato Si'*. Millions of people around the world have access to the homilies he preaches almost daily. The secular media have given him more attention by far than any other living religious leader. Over 40 million people follow his Twitter account. Parishes use material from the fourth chapter of his encyclical *Amoris Laetitia* in their marriage preparation programs. Many priests follow his advice on preaching in *The Joy of the Gospel (Evangelii Gaudium)* as they prepare their homilies. The documentary movie *Pope Francis: A Man of His Word*, by German filmmaker Wim Wenders, has given millions of viewers a flattering intimate picture of the pope. Through all these and many other pastoral activities, Pope Francis has made a significant impact on the Church and the larger world. He is revered by many as a moral compass for the human family, an authentic Christian believer, a compassionate pastor, and a pope dedicated to creating a more just, verdant, and peaceful world. At the same time, he has generated more public criticism than any other modern pope, as this book demonstrates.

The first chapter examines the most significant of the many five-year evaluations of the Francis papacy by journalists and theologians. The chapter begins by citing statistical studies of American attitudes toward Francis, showing that five years into his papacy, he had a remarkable 84 percent approval rating among U.S. Catholics.

In distinguishing evaluations of Francis, I use the terms *liberal* and *conservative*, borrowed from the political world and commonly applied to Church issues, realizing that they can mask important nuances. In general, conservatives fault Francis

Introduction

for sowing confusion in the Church on moral and doctrinal issues, while liberals laud him for renewing the spirit of Vatican II and applying Catholic social teaching to contemporary problems. In their five-year performance reviews, however, both groups were critical of the way Francis was handling the sex-abuse scandal. The first chapter includes my own generally positive view of Francis and most of his policies from two perspectives: one as a diocesan priest, who has spent fifty years trying to implement the Vatican II reforms and who appreciates the pope's efforts to revitalize the spirit of the Council, and the other as a theologian, heavily influenced by the German Jesuit Karl Rahner (1904–84), who sees Francis implementing Rahner's vision of a world Church.

The next five chapters consider specific issues by first establishing a context for the positions taken by Francis, and then noting specific criticisms and evaluating them. Chapter 2 places the position of Francis on gender issues in the context of a long history of patriarchal structures and sexist bias in society and the Church. Exceptions include the medieval mystic Hildegard of Bingen, who did a sophisticated analysis of male and female differences while maintaining that all the different characteristics are of equal value, and Karl Rahner, who insisted that the traditional arguments against women's ordination are not compelling. In line with the dominant tradition, Francis has maintained the teaching of Pope John Paul, ruling out women's ordination, but has given hope to his critics by initiating a study of the role of women deacons in the early Church and by expanding the role of women in the Church. The theory of gender complementarity, developed by the twentieth-century Swiss theologian Hans Urs von Balthasar, plays an important role in this chapter, since it has influenced the way Francis thinks about women and understands their role in the Church. The chapter ends with the hope that the Latin American pope will be guided by the Holy Spirit in his approach to gender issues.

The third chapter treats various issues that pertain to the economic realm. There is a short section on work that presents the thoughts of Francis as a challenge to high rates of unemployment and to workaholic tendencies. A section on business recalls the pope's general criticism of unbridled capitalism that has elicited strong rebuttals from conservative American economists who claim that Francis is overly influenced by Argentine crony capitalism and does not appreciate the effectiveness of free markets. In that debate, it is important to note that Francis speaks not as a trained economist but as a pastor concerned about poor and marginalized persons. The chapter also presents the pope's radical critique of consumerism and the technological paradigm that fosters it as well as his challenge to simplify our lifestyle. The final section on caring for the poor includes the call of Francis for a more equitable distribution of goods and wealth. Some American free-market economists argue that charitable giving is a better way of helping the poor than the "government redistribution" advocated by Francis. The pope's moral message on economic matters, which has drawn much criticism from conservative American economists, is a witness to the contemporary relevance of gospel values.

Chapter 4 highlights the authoritative teaching of Pope Francis that the liturgical reforms of Vatican II are "irrevocable." The great significance of this declaration comes to light in the context of the history of modern liturgical developments: the liturgical movement of the nineteenth and twentieth centuries; the reforms mandated by Vatican II; and the "reform the reform" movement led by Pope Benedict, who expanded opportunities for priests to celebrate the Tridentine Mass. American Catholics who are dissatisfied with the current English translation of the Mass will be pleased to note that Francis has reendorsed the Vatican II directive that national hierarchies are in charge of liturgical translations. The current main opposition to the pope's effort to make normative the Vatican II liturgical reforms comes from

Introduction

within the Curia, led by the prefect of the Congregation of Divine Worship, Cardinal Robert Sarah, who was appointed by Francis. The chapter recounts the ongoing dispute between Pope Francis and Cardinal Sarah with the hope that the pope's instruction will indeed revitalize contemporary liturgy.

The fifth chapter considers the volatile issue of communion for divorced and remarried Catholics. It summarizes and defends the teaching of the apostolic exhortation *Amoris Laetitia* that encourages persons in second marriages to engage in a prayerful personal discernment, in consultation with their pastors, on receiving communion at Mass. This approach is a wise pastoral strategy that views the goal of a loving, lifelong, monogamous marital partnership in the framework of a gospel ideal that is never totally achieved but compels continuing effort. Critics of Francis believe his approach sows confusion in the Church and threatens the traditional teaching on the indissolubility of a sacramental marriage. The chapter gives a good deal of attention to the book *To Change the Church* by Ross Douthat because of its potential influence in shaping negative public perceptions of Francis and his policies. Douthat, a columnist for the *New York Times*, claims that Francis has brought the Church to the edge of schism by his ambiguous statements on communion for remarried Catholics. *To Change the Church*, which has been reviewed in many influential publications, presents Francis as a reformist liberal pope constantly challenging traditional conservative Church teaching and practices. After summarizing Douthat's argument, the chapter presents some criticisms of his position, including my own view that his big picture narrative of an ongoing battle between liberals and conservatives lacks nuance and that his fear of schism is unfounded.

The last chapter on clergy sex abuse recounts the common negative evaluations of the way Francis handled the scandal during his first five years, including his distressing visit to Chile in January 2018. It also covers later developments: the apology of

Francis for mishandling the situation in Chile; his extended personal sessions with three victims; his three-day meeting with the Chilean bishops, all of whom offered to resign; and his acceptance of the resignation of Bishop Juan Barros, a central figure in the scandal, and four other bishops. The chapter summarizes the pope's letter to the people of God that serves as a response to the shocking grand jury report on clergy sex abuse in Pennsylvania. There is also a section analyzing the explosive public statements of Archbishop Carlo Vigano, charging Francis with ignoring the alleged sexual transgressions of Cardinal Theodore McCarrick. The chapter concludes with an analysis of the summit meeting in Rome designed to develop approaches to deal with the worldwide sex-abuse crisis.

The epilogue highlights the emphasis Pope Francis puts on synodality as the preferred approach to reforming the Church and making it a better instrument of spreading the kingdom.

1

FIVE-YEAR
ASSESSMENTS

The fifth anniversary of the March 13, 2013, election of Jorge Bergoglio as Bishop of Rome generated a great deal of valuable commentary on the pontificate of the first pope to come from Latin America, to belong to the Jesuit order, and to take the name Francis. It is helpful to keep in mind where Pope Francis stood with Americans five years into his papacy.

PEW STUDY

Shortly before the anniversary, the Pew Research Center published a well-respected study of how Pope Francis was perceived by U.S. Catholics and other citizens as well. At the time, 84 percent of American Catholics said they had a favorable view of Francis, with roughly 90 percent describing him as "compassionate" and "humble," and nearly 60 percent affirming him as "a major change" for the good. Among all citizens, including Catholics, around 60 percent had a favorable view of Francis.

At the same time, the study detected "signs of growing discontent with Francis on the political right," with 55 percent of Republican-leaning Catholics saying that the pope is "too liberal"

and 33 percent viewing him as "naive." These negative perceptions among Republican Catholics increased over four years: "too
liberal" by 32 percent and "naive" by 17 percent. At the same
time, their positive perceptions declined: overall approval was
down from 90 to 79 percent and "a positive force for change" was
down from 60 to 37 percent. During this same four-year period,
Democratic-leaning Catholics retained their generally positive
views of Francis with their favorability rating rising slightly from
87 to 89 percent, ten points higher than Republican Catholics.

COMMENTARIES

With these statistics in mind, let us review a sampling of
commentaries on the first five years of the Francis papacy, rang-
ing from harsh criticisms to predominately positive assessments.

First Things

The conservative journal *First Things* ran a series of articles
generally critical of Pope Francis. For instance, the March 27,
2017, article, "Pope Francis's Achilles Heel," by William Doino
Jr. elaborated on charges of what he called "weaknesses and dis-
appointments of this pontificate." Francis has not maintained "a
clear concept of Christian mercy," but stressed mercy to such a
degree that it gets disconnected from Christian truth and can be
used to "justify virtually any sin." The pope "has not emphasized
the danger of receiving Holy Communion unworthily," famously
insisting that the Eucharist is not "a prize for the perfect" but
a powerful medicine and nourishment for the weak without
warning the faithful about the serious dangers of a sacrilegious
communion. According to Doino, the pope has not explained or
defended his controversial teaching on communion for divorced
and remarried Catholics, leaving the Church with a "cacophony
of conflicting interpretations." He has refused requests to clarify

his teaching, allowing some to maintain that communion for those in irregular marriages is now legitimate. Furthermore, the article charged that the pope has not "checked the dissent and heterodoxy in the Church," allowing theologians to express heretical views, such as favoring women's ordination. Finally, Doino accused Francis of duplicity, saying one thing and doing another. He has, for example, advised pastors not to use "harsh and divisive language" but has called those who disagree with him "rigid," "legalistic," and "doctors of the law." Worse yet, Francis has not kept his promise to deal with clergy sex abuse, leaving the efforts at reform "in a state of disarray."

National Catholic Register

The conservative paper *National Catholic Register* published an editorial on March 12, 2018, claiming that Pope Francis has made a "mess" of things, bringing confusion into the Church during the first five years of his pontificate. The editorial is critical of his "extemporaneous messaging," especially his in-flight statements (e.g., "Who am I to judge?"), that prompt a "media frenzy" and create consternation among the faithful. The editors fault Francis for his "perceived slight of victims of sexual abuse" that damages his credibility. They contend that his attempt to normalize Vatican relations with China "has caused great alarm and confusion" among many who fear a betrayal of faithful Chinese Catholics. Their biggest concern is over the "contentious Chapter 8 that has been interpreted by some to open the door to Communion for divorced-and-remarried Catholics" and has created "irreconcilable differences among the world's bishops' conferences" over its pastoral application, increasing the confusion within the Catholic Church. The editorial concludes with a reminder that criticism of the pope "should be made with the spirit of humility that Francis himself emphasizes."

Ross Douthat

In his 2018 book, *To Change the Church: Pope Francis and the Future of Catholicism* (New York: Simon & Schuster), *New York Times* columnist Ross Douthat made the striking charge that Pope Francis has put the Church in danger of schism by his ambiguous teaching on communion for divorced and remarried Catholics. Since Douthat proposed a questionable grand narrative that received a good deal of attention in the secular world, I examine his book extensively in chapter 5 on communion for divorced and remarried Catholics.

Philip Lawler

Conservative journalist Philip Lawler provided another lengthy critique of Francis in his book *Lost Shepherd: How Pope Francis Is Misleading His Flock* (Washington, DC: Regnery Gateway, 2018). Lawler, who only gradually came to see the papacy of Francis as a "disaster," distinguishes his position from the "radical traditionalists," who contend that Francis is not really the pope, since either the position is now vacant or Benedict is the real pontiff. He does offer a series of criticisms of the pope's style, approach, and teaching. Francis's frequent "often damaging interviews produce journalistic sound bites," such as "Who am I to judge?" that cause confusion among the faithful. In some of his more formal statements, he is "out of his element," pronouncing on issues beyond his competency: for example, the dynamics of free-market capitalism and the reality of global warming. Furthermore, Francis's "environmental activism veered into doctrinal territory" when he proposed adding care for the environment to the traditional list of the corporal works of mercy, thus subverting their essential structure as person-to-person interactions.

When Francis addressed the U.S. Congress in 2015, Lawler noted that he never mentioned Jesus Christ, missing an opportunity to evangelize our leaders. His efforts to reform the Vatican finances have not borne much fruit because he did not do enough to support the good work of Cardinal Pell. Francis has not made ending the sex-abuse scandal a high priority. The pope was "a party to" the liberal manipulation of the Synod on the Family. In his apostolic exhortation *Amoris Laetitia*, the pope is deliberately vague on communion for remarried persons, thus accelerating "an already powerful trend to dismiss the Church's perennial teaching." In his public statements, Francis has become "increasingly strident, even insulting," frequently attacking "rigid" Christians who do not accept his reform agenda. In his peremptory dismissal of Cardinal Gerhard Müller from his post as prefect of the Congregation for the Doctrine of the Faith, the pope acted in a rude and insensitive way, contrary to his call for mercy and compassion in the Church. This pontificate has moved away from "an emphasis on the dignity of life and the integrity of the family, embracing instead the more popular causes of secular liberalism." The pope flouted liturgical directives by washing the feet of women on Holy Thursday. Contrary to the more open approach of his papal predecessors, John Paul and Benedict, Francis has "been careful to appoint cardinals who support his views," increasing the likelihood that the next pope will continue his policies. The pope refuses to "acknowledge the unique threat of Islamic terrorism," often insisting that Islam opposes violence. "By scorning tradition and scoffing at canon law," Francis has provoked divisions in the Church, broken the connection between generations of Catholics, devalued the work of his predecessors, and diminished the papal teaching office, making his papacy a "disaster for the Church."

In addition to this catalogue of papal missteps, Lawler worried about how Francis is going to handle Vatican relations with the People's Republic of China. For decades, the Holy See has been in a battle with the Communist Party, which insists on controlling the Church by appointing their own bishops to the Catholic Patriotic Association and refusing to recognize the underground bishops validly appointed by the Vatican. Many Chinese bishops have won approval of both the Chinese government and the Holy See. However, there is no agreed procedure on how to handle the naming of bishops. In the meantime, the government continues to make life difficult for faithful underground Catholics and to pressure valid bishops to join up with the Patriotic Association. Rumors are that the Vatican is ready to offer a compromise that allows Rome to appoint new bishops out of a list of candidates prepared by the Communist government. Cardinal Joseph Zen, the retired bishop of Hong Kong, fears the Vatican is going to make a bad agreement that excludes faithful priests from consideration for the episcopacy. Zen complains that he has sent letters to Francis about his concerns without getting any response. Echoing Cardinal Zen, Philip Lawler expressed his concerns that Pope Francis will be too eager to reach a deal, intimating that the pope may eventually betray faithful Chinese Catholics.

Commonweal

In a *Commonweal* article, "Five Years of Francis" (March 19, 2018), John Gehring, author of *The Francis Effect: A Radical Pope's Challenge to the American Catholic Church*, credits the pope for appointing U.S. bishops who recognize that being prolife means addressing issues beyond abortion and contraception, such as income inequality, climate change, and the treatment of immigrants. Francis has broadened the concerns of the American bishops to include economic justice, worker's rights, and gun control. In the Francis era, these issues can "no longer be regarded as peripheral, but as central to church teaching and Catholic identity." However, Gehring goes on to note the pope's "woefully insufficient response to clergy abuse," citing his mishandling of the situation in Chile and the lack of progress by the

Pontifical Commission for the Protection of Minors created by the pope in 2014. Gehring concludes, "Until Pope Francis can prove that he is up to the task of insuring a zero-tolerance policy toward abusive priests and creating real accountability for bishops, the promise of his remarkable papacy will be lost."

One month earlier, the February 6, 2018, issue of *Commonweal* ran an editorial highly critical of the way Pope Francis has handled the sex-abuse scandal. The editors suggested that, at the five-year mark of his papacy, it is time to recognize the limitations of his "free-wheeling style," his "off-the-cuff remarks to the press," "his parallel information structure," and his tendency to rely "on an informal network of informants and his own instincts rather than structured briefings." This style makes accountability difficult and neglects the need for structural change. The editorial is critical of the way Francis has handled the sex-abuse problem in Chile, appointing Juan Barros as bishop of Osorno against the advice of the Chilean bishops' conference and, in an airplane interview, dismissing charges against Barros as "calumny," which the editors called "a shocking, incredible statement without proof." They went on to claim that these actions "reveal the shortcomings of Francis's impatience with established procedures and the unglamorous business of steering a sclerotic bureaucracy."

Massimo Faggioli

Writing for *La Croix International*, theologian Massimo Faggioli highlighted in "Synodality and Its Perils" (April 3, 2018) the efforts of Pope Francis to make the Synod of Bishops, established by Paul VI in 1965, a more effective instrument for Church renewal. Francis wants a "synodal church," which models "participation, solidarity and transparency." He is "not afraid to let the people be active participants in the ecclesial process." He encouraged a broad consultation for the 2014 and 2015 Synods on the Family and again for the 2018 Synod on Youth, Faith, and

Vocational Discernment. For Faggioli, the pope's use of the synodal process on Church issues has a broader significance, serving as a model for constitutional democracies facing the same critical challenge of how to represent their people more effectively. Furthermore, successful ecclesial synods make the institutional church more credible and less susceptible to "neo-traditionalist critics," who "question the credibility of Pope Francis's representative role in the church" and challenge his reforms. During his first five years, Francis has made only "baby steps" toward greater participation in the life of the Church, but this sets the stage, according to Faggioli, for further progress toward a more representative synodal Church.

Time Magazine

In February 2018, *Time* magazine ran an article by Christopher Hale, "Pope Francis's Failure to Address Abuse Allegations Jeopardizes the Papacy," that begins with praise for the pope, who has advanced "an agenda of reform" touching nearly "every corner of the Catholic Church" from the "new focus on the environment and the poor to an emphasis on simplicity and sobriety among the clergy." Hale, a supporter of Francis, insists, however, that all this good will be "for naught" and that his papacy will be a "tragic failure" if the pope does not "transform his focus and practice on ending the systematic cover-up of sexual abuse in the Catholic Church."

America Magazine

Likewise, in "Five Years into Pope Francis' Papacy, There Is Much More Noise to Be Made" published on March 5, 2018, the editors of the Jesuit review *America* noted positive accomplishments of the first Jesuit pope: modeling a simple lifestyle; advocating for the poor, the marginalized people, and the victims of a throwaway culture; condemning war, unfettered markets, and growing economic disparity; voicing moral concerns to international leaders, including President Trump; producing three landmark documents, *Evangelii Gaudium*, *Laudato Si'*, and *Amoris Laetitia*; and promoting an ecclesiology of communion that respects national hierarchies and indigenous cultures. These positive developments make more painful the "uneven response" of the pope to clerical sex abuse, especially since those abused are some of the "most obvious victims of the throwaway culture Francis condemns."

Gerard O'Connell, Vatican correspondent for *America*, recognized the "utmost importance" of the sex-abuse issue, but insisted that the papacy of Francis should be judged not just on a single failure, but also on a string of successes: fostering a missionary spirit in the Church; energizing the Church by his focus on mercy; emphasizing the peripheries by visiting thirty-three countries and creating cardinals from around the world; revitalizing the spirit of Vatican II by applying the gospel to contemporary issues in his writings and especially his homilies; demystifying the papacy by his simple lifestyle and admission of personal limitations; promoting ecumenical and interfaith dialogue and collaboration; promoting justice and peace; beginning a reform of the Curia so it serves the local churches, although much more needs to be done; creating a more welcoming atmosphere for bishops making their regularly scheduled visits to Rome and providing opportunity for them to have extended dialogue with the pope; appointing some women to official positions in major Vatican departments, with more to come; calling a 2018 Synod of Bishops on Young People; and preparing for World Youth Day in Panama during January 2019. O'Connell recognized that Francis has not done well on the sex-abuse scandal and has much more to do on other matters, such as the role of women, reform of the Curia, and Vatican relations with China. He remained optimistic, however, that Pope Francis will leave "a pontificate of seeds," setting in motion reforms that need time to mature and will be harvested by his successors.

Joan Chittister

Writing in the newspaper *National Catholic Reporter* as part of its "Francis at Five Series," Joan Chittister, OSB, argued that the papacy of Francis has stalled, run out of energy. He has promised much with little results, making the current situation even more disappointing. Five years ago, Francis did introduce a new style of papal leadership, helping us see the Church as a sign of God's love rather than a specter of divine wrath. He presented himself as a humble man in need of prayers, advised bishops to come out of their offices and walk with their people, reminded priests to proclaim God's mercy in the sacrament of penance, sent a positive signal to the gay community, alerted the world to the plight of migrants and refugees, and said a definitive no to nuclear weapons. According to Chittister, Francis has not, however, done enough to make real progress on important issues, such as restoring the female deaconate, calling to account bishops and priests complicit in sex abuse, and promoting women to leadership roles in the Church. For Chittister, real reform in the Church comes from the base, from faithful people living the gospel daily. Nevertheless, popes and bishops can affect the tone and effectiveness of the Church by exercising their leadership in an open, empathic, and loving manner. In the case of Pope Francis, his style and statements have generated high hopes of renewal that have been frustrated, leading to, as Chittister put it, "long-term distrust" and even greater disappointment.

The Catholic Herald

Writing for the British online publication *The Catholic Herald*, in the article "Pope Francis's Bold Reforms Have Been

Frustrated. How Did This Happen?" (February 2, 2018), Ed Condon, a canon lawyer and supporter of Pope Francis, asked why his "big and bold" reforms have achieved so little in the first five years of his pontificate. The Council of Cardinals set up by Francis has "yet to produce anything of substance." Despite the pope's efforts to bring accountability to the curial finances and the Vatican Bank, "financial scandals remain a depressingly fixed feature of Vatican life." His attempts to establish institutional structures to deal with the clergy sex-abuse scandal "have not yet gained much traction." The pope's "instincts are right" and his leadership is "bold and dynamic," but "nothing appears to be changing." Condon blamed this on the pope's personal style; for instance, relying on a few close advisors and informal meetings, which is "simply not yielding results." "Those currently charged with implementing his reforms seem unable or unwilling to see them through." According to Condon, Francis can still accomplish his important reforms if he puts more emphasis on "proper process, scrupulous respect for the law, and a zeal for the sometimes-tedious minutiae of getting things done."

New York Times

The April 29, 2018, *New York Times* carried an article by Jason Horowitz titled "Pope Francis in the Wilderness," which recalled the pope's election as an agent of change and recognized the strong conservative criticisms of the "increasingly embattled" pope. He added, however, that a close look at the record shows Francis continues to get his way in reorienting the Church by prioritizing "social justice issues over culture war issues such as abortion." Horowitz buys the notion, expressed by others, that Francis is winning the battle with his conservative critics and that the longer his pontificate continues, the more likely his reforms will be irreversible.

In the larger geopolitical world, Horowitz pointed out that the pro-immigration policies of Francis put him in opposition to powerful nationalist trends around the world. While the pope sees migrants as the primary victims of globalization, nationalist leaders, on both sides of the Atlantic, including President Trump, view them as a "hostile, unsettling force" and want to keep them out of their countries. Horowitz noted that supporters of Francis think that his experience with Argentine populism prepared him to meet the challenges of economic globalization and political nationalism and to "appreciate the grievances of frustrated and unemployed workers." The article concluded that Francis "seems comfortable with his new role as a lone voice in the populist wilderness," suggesting that the pope is playing the role of a true prophet who speaks the truth and "puts himself on the line."

EVALUATING CONSERVATIVE COMMENTARIES

The 2018 Pew report provides perspective for evaluating various commentaries on the first five years of the Francis pontificate. Reading just the conservative publications could, for example, give the impression of widespread discontent with the first Latin American pope. However, the report, which shows a remarkable 84 percent approval rating for Francis, suggests that the vociferous critics, who get a lot of attention, represent, in fact, the views of a small percentage of American Catholics, especially since some of the disapproval of the pope comes from liberals who want more progressive reforms. The partisan differential revealed by the Pew study (55 percent of Republicans say Francis is too liberal compared to 19 percent of Democrats) reminds us of the growing influence of party politics on all phases of American life and suggests that the pope's moral pronouncements on issues, such as capitalism, immigration, and climate change, are perceived by some conservatives as unwarranted intrusions into the political arena beyond his competency. The Pew Report indicated that only 2 percent of Catholics think their pastors are opposed to Francis, suggesting that priests inspired by John Paul and Benedict either hide their displeasure with Francis or appreciate some aspects of his style and teaching. Regardless, the polling shows no signs of a clergy rebellion against Pope Francis. My own anecdotal perception is that the divide between spiritual-father priests and servant-leader priests has been less contentious under Francis than during the Benedict years.

CONSERVATIVE CONCERNS

Many of the conservative critics of the Francis papacy noted their initial positive response to his early symbolic expressions of a simple lifestyle and a ministry of humble service. Some continued to find positive aspects of his ministry and teaching. For example, Philip Lawler, admits that, in parts of *Amoris Laetitia,* Francis "shows his true character as a pastor; encouraging, guiding, questioning, cajoling, sympathizing, instructing, helping readers to gain a deeper appreciation for the Church's understanding of sacramental marriage" (*Lost Shepherd*, 117). For the most part, however, the conservative commentators gradually became disenchanted with Francis and more critical of his statements and policies. Their common complaint is that Francis has brought confusion into the Church, especially by his statements that seem to question traditional teaching on specific issues, such as homosexuality and the indissolubility of sacramental marriage. Conservative critics in the United States, where climate change is such a divisive political issue, are united in condemning the pope for taking sides on the supposedly disputed scientific issue of anthropogenic global warming. Most are also critical of the way Francis has handled the sex-abuse scandal and the reform of the Curia. There is growing agreement among them that Francis is too harsh on his opponents, often describing them in derogatory language. Their biggest concern, however, is that the pope, in opening the possibility of communion for remarried Catholics, has effectively undercut the traditional teaching on the indissolubility of sacramental marriage.

CONSERVATIVE OVERREACTIONS

As a supporter of Francis and most of his policies, I believe many of the conservative criticisms are overdrawn or misplaced. There really is no widespread confusion among Catholics, as the Pew report makes clear. The pope has not denied any Church teaching and has, on numerous occasions, affirmed the traditional opposition to abortion, contraception, and gay marriage. In taking a position on climate change, Francis did not claim any scientific expertise, but relied on recent studies, including the consensus developed by the prestigious Pontifical Academy of Science. The pope generally does not name his critics but has denounced modern-day Pharisees and "Doctors of the Law" who close the doors of the Church to those who wish to enter. Significantly, he included himself in asking for prayers that "we shepherds" not "close the door" to those seeking a closer relationship with the Church. The conservative criticisms of Francis on clergy sex abuse during his first five years deserve serious consideration. They must also be seen in the light of further developments, as we will see in chapter 6.

Chapter 5 will deal extensively with the radical claims of Ross Douthat that Francis has brought the Church to the edge of schism, but here, we can at least say that today there are no signs of a pending rupture of Church unity. Cardinal Raymond Burke and his fellow cardinals, who are so critical of Pope Francis, have made it clear that they do not intend to separate from the Church. It is true that a few American bishops and priests are openly critical of Francis while others express their opposition privately.

Nevertheless, American bishops, as a whole, remain loyal to Rome and have no thoughts of leading a schism. It is also true that wealthy and influential laypersons have control of large media outlets that regularly criticize Francis and his reform efforts. However, even radical traditionalist groups in the United States have not threatened to leave the Church, preferring instead to deny that Francis is really the pope. Worry about schism simply misreads the reality of Church life today.

EVALUATING LIBERAL COMMENTARIES

The liberal commentators found much to like in their five-year assessment of the Francis pontificate. They applaud his appointment of the Council of Cardinals to advise on governing the Church, though they tend to be critical of a lack of progress. His major writings, *Evangelii Gaudium*, *Laudato Si'*, and *Amoris Laetitia*, have received favorable liberal reviews. On the international stage, they credit Francis with promoting peace and justice, assisting refugees, and supporting the Paris Agreement. On Church matters, they are pleased with his appointment of cardinals and bishops, his revival of the spirit of Vatican II, and his authoritative support for the Vatican II liturgical reforms. Liberals are generally disappointed, however, that Francis has not done more to increase the role of women in the Church. Some join the conservative critics in pointing out problems with the pope's informal leadership style, especially bypassing the Curia in seeking reforms that require institutional implementation. Even the most positive commentators were critical of the pope's failure during his first five years to address adequately the sex-abuse crisis, some claiming that it vitiates all the good he has done on other issues.

Although much of the liberal evaluation of the first five years of the Francis pontificate is on target, it seems an overreaction to claim that the positive accomplishments of Francis will be negated if he continues to fail to make significant progress on the sex-abuse scandal, as utterly disappointing as that would be. Contemporary Christian anthropologies have moved beyond the scholastic notion that a person should be judged evil if they have any serious moral defect. The notion of "fundamental option" proposed by moral theologians means that persons who, in the core of their being, strive to do God's will are not essentially compromised by one or the other aspects of their life not completely under the sway of their option for good. Applying these theological insights, which challenge all forms of "all-or-nothing" thinking, to the Francis papacy, we can presume that his great accomplishments are not totally vitiated by any of his failures. Practically, his appointment of pastoral cardinals and bishops, for instance, will have an ongoing positive effect no matter how limited or flawed his efforts to deal with other issues such as reform of the Curia, the role of women, and the sex-abuse scandal.

HISTORICAL DEVELOPMENTS

Five-year evaluations can be very revealing but have obvious limitations. History, which is created by the ongoing interaction between God's self-communication and human responses, often produces surprising developments. The essentially unknowable future, which relentlessly becomes the present, interprets the past, illuminating the often-hidden dynamic interplay of grace and sin that characterizes the human adventure. When we come to the end of the papacy of Francis, we will have a better sense of the successes and failures of the early years than we have now. Historians will then continue the process of judging the significance of decisions made and directions charted by Pope Francis.

We already have an important example of such historical development. Just months after commentators universally condemned

Francis for his treatment of the sex-abuse issue in Chile, he took some constructive steps to deal with the problem that may prove to be a significant development in his ongoing treatment of the horrendous scandal that hangs heavy over the whole Church. Chapter 6 of this book will examine that issue more closely.

A PASTORAL PERSPECTIVE

From my perspective as a diocesan priest, ordained in 1962, just months before the beginning of Vatican II, the Francis pontificate appears as a revitalization of the heady days of the Council and the early years of applying its spirit and teachings to the challenges of everyday pastoral ministry. Francis has renewed the dream of a new Pentecost articulated so eloquently by Pope John XXIII at the beginning of the Council. Our first Latin American pope has refocused our attention on the great conciliar themes that gave early shape and direction to pastoral ministry: the Church as the people of God; priests as servant leaders; laypersons called to holiness; full, active, conscious participation in the liturgy, the font of the Christian life; positive evaluations of other religions and the importance of dialogue and collaboration; salvation optimism; religious liberty for all; Church as a sign and instrument of the kingdom of God; scripture as the normative source of spiritual nourishment and moral guidance; and the Church as leaven for humanizing culture and creating a more just society. Francis has demonstrated once again the power and joy of the simple unadorned gospel message. He has reignited enthusiasm for the conciliar reforms, often thwarted by various "reform of the reform" movements. Pope Francis has not only generated renewed hope and energy for older Catholics formed by Vatican II, but also provided younger generations with an inspiring vision and practical wisdom on the enduring challenge of building up the Body of Christ and spreading the reign of God in the world. Although there is now no empirical evidence of a widespread Francis effect on the Catholic practice of the faith, history will reveal if the seeds the pope has planted will have an impact on future generations of Catholics.

A RAHNERIAN PERSPECTIVE

As a theologian steeped in the thought of the influential German Jesuit theologian Karl Rahner (1904–84), I see the first Jesuit pope making significant strides toward the world Church envisioned by Rahner. In the late 1970s, Rahner proposed his interpretation of Vatican II, not so much as the culmination of liturgical, theological, and ecumenical movements, but as the tiny beginning of a new era when the Church will for the first time explicitly understand itself as a world Church. In this development, rivalled in importance only by the Council of Jerusalem in AD 49 that admitted Gentile converts without demanding they accept and practice Judaism, the Church will function like a communion of local churches, all rooted in their native cultures. The world Church will not be dominated by European and American bishops, and it will not function like an export firm disseminating a Vatican version of Christianity around the globe. The Second Vatican Council (1962–65) did exhibit certain intimations of a world Church: bishops from Asia and Africa were active participants; local churches were given permission to celebrate liturgy in their vernacular languages; the Pastoral Constitution addressed the entire human family with all its joys and sorrows; council documents offered a positive assessment of the world religions, spoke of salvation for all who follow their conscience, promoted interfaith and ecumenical dialogue, and supported freedom of conscience for all. In the world Church, the Bishop of Rome will be in dialogue with other religious leaders. National conferences of bishops will assume greater authority to make regional adaptations. Vatican curial officials will not dictate norms and policies to local churches but will serve their needs. Liturgical celebrations will more clearly represent the best of local cultures. Ecumenical and interfaith dialogue will search for a deeper understanding of the truth. The Vatican will no longer impose a uniform Canon Law on local churches. The Catholic Church will collaborate with other spiritual traditions in the effort to create a more just and peaceful world.

From this Rahnerian perspective, the papacies of John Paul and Benedict impeded the transition to a world Church in important ways: for example, limiting the power of national hierarchies and giving the Curia control over liturgical translations. In contrast, Francis has made many moves that contribute to the greater development of the world Church envisioned by Rahner. He created the Council of Cardinals, representing various geographical regions of the world, thereby symbolizing and actualizing the mission of the Church to evangelize all people. He often quotes national conferences of bishops in his writings, indicating that all wisdom does not reside in Rome. He has returned final authority in liturgical translations to regional hierarchies, thus limiting the power of the Curia and respecting the obvious competency of local experts. His appointments of new cardinals from around the world ensures worldwide participation in the election of the next pope. His humble recognition that he does not have all the answers to regional problems encourages local leaders to assume greater responsibility for applying the gospel to their unique situations. His emphasis on the fundamental gospel message sets the stage for evangelizing that allows Christianity to incorporate the best of local cultures. His insistence on personal prayerful discernment of moral responsibilities encourages respect for unique situations that differ in various cultures and societies. In my own evaluation of the Francis pontificate to this point, the first Jesuit pope deserves great credit for taking specific, concrete steps toward implementation of the Rahnerian dream of a world Church more reflective of the universal message of Christ that can take root and grow in all cultures.

2

GENDER ISSUES

HISTORY OF SEXISM

A friendly critic suggested that when Pope Francis discusses gender issues, he sounds like an eighty-year-old Latin American male. This quip reminds us that we should examine the pope's positions on gender in various contexts, including the history of his Catholic heritage.

Bible

The Bible, which is normative for Christians, was written entirely by men in patriarchal cultures and often betrays a sexist bias. The Book of Genesis, for instance, records the story of Abraham, the great patriarch, palming his wife, Sarah, off as his sister to King Abimelech in order to save himself but exposing Sarah to sexual exploitation (Gen 20:1–17). In the Letter to the Ephesians, the sexist bias is more explicit: "Wives, be subject to your husbands as you are to the Lord. For the husband is the head of the wife just as Christ is the head of the church, the body of which he is the savior" (Eph 5:22–23).

Note that Pope Francis is very aware of scriptural passages that subvert the general patriarchal thrust of the Bible. The Book of Genesis, for example, suggests a fundamental equality between men and women since God created them in his own image and likeness, "male and female he created them" (Gen 1:27–28). The Apostle Paul grounded gender equality in our fundamental relationship to Christ: "There is no longer Jew or Greek, there is no longer slave or free, there is no longer male and female; for all of you are one in Christ Jesus" (Gal 3:28).

Mary of Magdala is a great example of rising above biblical cultural norms. Cured of a serious illness by Jesus, this Galilean woman accompanied him on his journey to Jerusalem and was present at his crucifixion, while the male disciples fled. According to John, the risen Christ first appeared to Mary and sent her to the disciples to report the good news, which has earned her the title "Apostle to the Apostles" and made her a prominent figure in discussions of the role of women in the Church.

Church Fathers

The writings of the Church fathers, both East and West, contain strong misogynistic statements: for example, Origen (d. 254), the great representative of Eastern Orthodox theology, insisted that women not speak in public assemblies, even if they had valuable things to contribute, precisely because they are women, who are always a threat to lure men into sin. In the West, Augustine (d. 430) wrote, "What is the difference whether it is in a wife or a mother, it is still Eve the temptress that we must beware of in any woman…. I fail to see what use women can be to men, if one excludes the function of having children." There are exceptions to this sexist bias. St. Gregory Nazianzus (d. 390), for instance, defended women's rights by insisting that both men and women possess an equal dignity because both are made in the image and likeness of God.

Medieval Period

During the medieval period, Thomas Aquinas (d. 1274) accepted Aristotle's notion that females are misbegotten males, lacking the fullness of humanity, meaning that women are essentially inferior to men and should therefore be subject to them. He used this same questionable analysis to explain why women could not be ordained priests. In the late Middle Ages, Martin Luther (d. 1546), who made a happy marriage with Katie von Bora, repeated Augustine's charge that women lead men into sin: It is you women "with your tricks and artifices that lead men into error."

An important exception to medieval patriarchy is the talented, creative mystic Hildegard of Bingen (d. 1179), who developed a sophisticated analysis of four types of male and female behavior and how they interact. Based on erroneous biology but insightful psychology, she distinguished male and female types, in part, according to the intensity of the sexual drive and the ability to form chaste friendships. Furthermore, she accepted the existence of distinctive sexual characteristics: for instance, men show courage and strength while women demonstrate mercy and grace. Anticipating an emphasis in modern psychology, she encouraged each sex to develop the other sex's main characteristics: men showing more compassion and women more fortitude. What distinguishes Hildegard's analysis, however, is her insistence that these distinctive characteristics are of equal value. As made in the image of God, men and women are inherently equal. Their sexual differences are not polarizing but complementary. Hildegard of Bingen stands as a reminder that we Christians today are not trapped in the world of traditional patriarchy but are free to find new ways for men and women to relate based on respect and equality.

Hans Urs von Balthasar

In the twentieth century, Swiss theologian Hans Urs von Balthasar (1905–88) proposed his own version of gender complementarity that makes the ordination of women metaphysically impossible. For Balthasar, the gender differences between males and females, evident in human reproduction, are normative for all interactions between men and women. In sexual intercourse, men are the active agent and women are, as Balthasar puts it, "active recipients." Although he often insists on the fundamental equality of the sexes, the Swiss theologian gives primacy to the male role and limits the role of females. Gender is an important category throughout his theology. The human family is feminine (actively receptive) in relation to the God active in history. The Church is feminine, the bride, in relation to Christ, the bridegroom, who actively sustains the community of faith. In this regard, he proposed the so-called iconic argument that only males could be priests since they represent the active male Christ in relation to the Church. Women cannot be priests because they are by nature active recipients and cannot be conformed to Christ, the head of the Body. Furthermore, Balthasar insisted that the Church must be a bulwark against a feminism that denies all sexual differences. In response, feminist theologians insist that his iconic argument unfairly identifies women with their reproductive role and limits their participation in the public life of the Church and society.

John Paul II

Between 1979 and 1984, Pope John Paul II gave a series of 129 lectures on human sexuality that were compiled and published as *The Joy of the Body: Human Love in the Divine Plan* (1997). The pope presents a positive understanding of sexuality that sees the human body as a sacrament of divine revelation. He challenges the cultural assumption that sex is an autonomous possession to be used for personal self-gratification. His theory of gender complementarity echoes themes found in von Balthasar, without any explicit attribution. Anatomical differences and reproductive sex make women fundamentally receptive of male activity. Marital intercourse, which involves total self-giving, serves as a metaphor for the divine human relationship in which God is the active agent and we humans are recipients of divine love. John Paul often stresses the fundamental equality of men and women, but in their interactions, women are the receptive partner. The pope consistently praises women for their distinctive contributions as mothers, which identifies them with their domestic role while downplaying their participation in public life. He opposes forms of feminism that seek to make women "like men."

John Paul II uses a form of the iconic argument to insist that women cannot be ordained priests. In presiding at the Eucharist, the priest takes the place of Christ and acts in his person. Sacraments require a natural resemblance between the sign and the one signified. Therefore, only males can properly preside at Mass because only they can adequately symbolize Christ, who is the active agent in sanctifying the feminine receptive church. In his 1994 apostolic letter *Ordinatio Sacerdotalis*, John Paul praised women and their contributions to Church and society but then explicitly declared, "The church has no authority whatsoever to confer priestly ordination on women," thus attempting to eliminate further debate.

The pope's apostolic letter, however, did not halt discussion of women's ordination among all segments of the Catholic community and raised further questions about the binding character of his prohibition. In November 1995, the Congregation for the Doctrine of the Faith (CDF), headed by Cardinal Ratzinger, issued a statement declaring that the teaching of John Paul does belong to the deposit of faith and requires definitive assent because it is "founded on the written word of God" and "has been set forth infallibly by the ordinary and universal magisterium." This statement by the CDF, meant to silence dissent on this volatile topic, has not won total acceptance since some theologians continue to debate it, and a majority of U.S. Catholics still favor women's ordination.

Karl Rahner

In examining the historical context for discussing the gender questions, including women's ordination, it is helpful to recall the response of the German Jesuit theologian Karl Rahner (1904–84) to a 1976 declaration of the CDF forbidding women's ordination, which employed the same general line of argument as their 1994 declaration. Rahner, who was very sensitive to discrimination against women in the Church and society, challenged the argument that the practice of Jesus and the Apostles, which did not include women in the official leadership of the Twelve, is normative for all succeeding historical periods. He argued that the fundamental principle of male and female equality, implicit in the teaching of Jesus, did not immediately challenge the entrenched patriarchal structures of his society. The position of women in Jewish culture of the day made it virtually impossible for them to be among the Twelve, the official witnesses for the life, death, and resurrection of Jesus. This presents an adequate explanation for the practice of Jesus and the Apostolic Church, which excluded women from official leadership positions both in Jewish and Greco-Roman communities. According to Rahner, this means that the exclusionary practice of the early Church is not necessarily normative for later historical periods like our own. He thinks it is significant that the fathers of the Church and the medieval theologians argued against women's ordination based on women's inferiority and not on gospel teaching. Rahner claims the same dynamics have been at work regarding the question of slavery. The fundamental Christian principle that all humans have equal dignity and worth did not immediately challenge the institution of slavery, but only achieved its societal application in the last few centuries with the abolition of slavery in the developed world. Rahner contends that with the modern progress on women's rights, the burden of proof is now on the Vatican to explain why women should be excluded from the priesthood. Despite the more recent statements by the CDF, theologians, men and women, have continued to use Rahner-type arguments in favor of women's ordination in the Catholic Church.

POPE FRANCIS

This background helps us understand the position of Pope Francis, the first Jesuit Bishop of Rome. On a flight from Sweden to Rome in November 2016, Francis, responding to a journalist's question, said, "On the ordination of women in the Catholic Church, the last word is clear," referring to the absolute prohibition stated by John Paul in his 1994 apostolic letter. Pressed whether this prohibition was forever, Francis replied, "It goes in that direction."

He went on to speak positively about the role of women in the Church, insisting that "women can do many other things better than men." For him, the Marian or "feminine dimension" of the Church is more important in the theology and spirituality of the Church than the Petrine apostolic dimension led by the bishops. This last comment, which reflects the ecclesiology of von Balthasar, raises the question of the position of Francis on gender complementarity. He has expressed his opposition to the gender theory taught in schools that denies or downplays sexual differences. In that regard, he has said, "I am in support of women, yes! But feminism, no." Furthermore, "We must not fall into the trap of feminism, because this would reduce the importance of women." More positively, the pope insists, "The way of viewing a problem, of seeing things, is different in a woman compared to a man. They must be complimentary, and in consultation, it is important that there are women." Again reflecting von Balthasar, Francis says, "The consecrated woman is an icon of the Church, an icon of Mary," while the priest is an icon of the apostles, who were sent to preach. Women can preach in many settings, according to Francis, but not at the eucharistic liturgy where the priest presides in the person of Christ. Using the nuptial imagery favored by Pope John Paul, Francis speaks of the Church as the Bride of Christ, married to the Lord, her bridegroom, adding that women, with their "feminine genius," symbolize this relationship, while men do not.

Feminist Criticism

The fundamental problem, identified by many critics, with the gender complementarity espoused by von Balthasar, John Paul, and Francis is that it tends to identify women with their reproductive role and domestic responsibilities while limiting their public role in the Church and society. It rules out women's ordination and limits their power in the Church. While praising the "feminine genius," it makes women essentially dependent, recipients of male activity.

Feminist scholars have collected quotes from Francis that suggest his tendency to identify women with childbearing and his insensitivity to real concerns of contemporary women. Noting the need for more women theologians, Francis describes them as "the strawberries on the cake, but there is a need for more." Addressing a group of vowed religious: "The consecrated woman must be a mother and not an old maid." While advocating for a greater role for women in the Church, he added, "I am wary of a solution that can be reduced to a kind of female machismo." Addressing the European Parliament, he compared a culturally weary Europe to a grandmother who is "no longer fertile or vibrant." Feminist theologians point out that Francis, along with many other men generally sympathetic to the cause of women, does not really understand how his language offends women and limits their public role by identifying them with childbearing.

In addition to these critics who are disappointed in Pope Francis for not moving forward on women's ordination and for accepting a flawed version of gender complementarity, members of the LGBT community have criticized the pope for not explicitly repudiating the teaching of Pope Benedict, found also in the *Catechism*, that same-sex inclinations are "objectively disordered." They also claim Francis has not been strong enough in his defense of gay persons, especially in his exhortation *Amoris Laetitia*, which they see as weaker than the synod report that it reflects.

Defenders of Francis

Pope Francis, who remains very popular among U.S. Catholics, has important defenders on gender issues. Some women theologians have said the pope is so good on so many other issues that they are willing to give him a pass on this one. Other Catholic scholars have argued that his position on gender complementarity is less rigid and more nuanced than his papal predecessors. Francis has a strong sense of the Holy Spirit, who is the source of unity, harmony, and fundamental equality in human relationships. He understands that male-female relationships are influenced by diverse societal norms and cultural patterns, which are a mix of grace and patriarchal sexism. His pastoral practice of walking with those struggling to live the Christian life makes him attentive to the cause of women who seek a greater role in Church and society. It seems the position of Francis on gender complementarity is at least open to developments that would be more congenial to the concerns of his critics.

Interestingly, some secular commentators have come to the defense of Francis, noting that his ecclesial critics are so focused on the ordination issue that they fail to appreciate the great things he has done for women worldwide. His recognition that we are facing a unified ecological crisis that threatens the earth and the poor is crucial for the well-being of women who are among the least prepared to defend themselves and their children from this threat. The pope's personal integrity and authenticity implicitly challenge misogyny and sexism. Finally, some of the secular commentators have praised Francis for halting the questionable investigation of U.S. women religious, which has opened the door to greater roles for women in the Church.

Just as critics of Francis have assembled a series of unfavorable quotes on women, so it is possible to find more favorable statements. "We need more women theologians." "We need to create still broader opportunities for a more inclusive feminine presence in the Church." "Why is it taken for granted that women must earn less than men? No! They have the same rights. The discrepancy is a pure scandal." There is "a radical equality between spouses." "The role of women in the church must not be limited to being mothers, workers, a limited role....No! It is something more." "Women, in the Church, are more important than bishops and priests: how, this is something we have to try to explain better, because I believe that we lack a theological explanation of this." All these quotes need the context to grasp their full impact, but just standing alone they suggest that Francis wants to champion the rights of women and to expand their role in society and Church, even if critics detect his limited perspective on the problem in these statements. In this regard, Francis has appointed at least four women to important positions in the Roman Curia, and in a historic, unprecedented move, he named three women scholars as consultors to the Congregation for the Doctrine of the Faith.

Women Deacons

In August 2016, Pope Francis appointed six men and six women to study the issue of women deacons and their ministry, especially in the early Church. In 2002, the International Theological Commission issued a report that recognized the existence of female deacons in the early Church but indicated their role could not be simply equated with male deacons. The U.S. theologian Phyllis Zagano, one of the twelve appointed by Francis, has argued for a more positive reading of history that suggests the possibility of ordaining women deacons today. According to Zagano, women were ordained deacons in the Church from the earliest days into the Middle Ages, and the ordination ritual was the same as for men. In Romans, Paul refers to Phoebe as a deacon (Rom 16:1). The Council of Chalcedon (451), echoing Nicaea (325), speaks of bishops "laying hands on her," a reference to ordaining women deacons. The Eastern Church has a long history of women deacons and has recently considered reinstating the practice. The German bishops have asked Vatican permission to ordain women deacons several times since 1975. Finally, Zagano points out that most Catholics are open to women deacons, who would enrich the ministry of the Church. After two years, the commission has yet to report significant progress. Nevertheless, the study continues, giving hope that, under the guidance of the Holy Spirit, it will eventually produce results favorable to the role of women in the Church.

The LGBT Community

Although some critics have faulted Francis for his limited support of the LGBT community, others have praised him for his explicit comments defending gay persons. He has clearly stated that homosexuals "should not be discriminated against" and deserve respect and pastoral care. He has also said, "I think that the Church not only should apologize to a gay person whom it offended" but also "must ask for forgiveness, not just say sorry." For the pope, "people should not be defined by their sexual tendencies; let us not forget that God loves all his creatures." Commenting on his now famous question, "Who am I to judge?" Francis said he was paraphrasing the *Catechism*, which insists that homosexual persons "should be treated with dignity and not be marginalized."

His positive public interactions with LGBT persons, for example, embracing a gay couple during his visit to Washington, reinforce his consistent support of persons with diverse sexual orientations. Another significant example comes from Chilean sex-abuse survivor Juan Cruz, who revealed his homosexual orientation to Francis and reported the pope's affirming response: "God made you like this and loves you like this. The pope loves you like this. You have to be happy with who you are."

Pope Francis is indeed an older Latin American male who sometimes speaks in a way that betrays the patriarchal bias of his culture. He is also a loyal son of the Church who is faithful to previous teachings. At the same time, he is a compassionate pastor who tries to walk with persons who are hurting and feel alienated from the Church. He also recognizes that the Church must always be reforming itself and that there is a proper development of Church teaching and practice. It will be interesting to see how the Church develops on gender issues under the leadership of Pope Francis. There are clues. He has given no realistic hope to his critics who are passionate about ordaining women to the priesthood. He has initiated a process that could lead to the ordination of women deacons and has taken concrete steps to expand the role of women in the Church. At least, his theory of gender complementarity is open to development and does not necessarily curtail the participation of women in public affairs. In general, the LGBT community enjoys the support of Francis and can hope that he will soften the harsh language found in the *Catechism*. As to further developments, we do well to stay open to the promptings of the Holy Spirit, as Pope Francis reminds us.

3

ECONOMIC ISSUES

SPIRITUALITY OF WORK

In his encyclical *Laudato Si'* (*LS*), Pope Francis insists that an "integral ecology," designed to care for the earth and the poor, needs a "correct understanding of work," which includes all purposeful human activity, manual and mental, involving a "modification of existing reality" (no. 125). Drawing on the wisdom of Pope John Paul II in his encyclical *Laborem Exercens*, Francis notes that God placed Adam and Eve in the garden not only to preserve it but also to make it fruitful (Gen 2:15). This suggests that we ourselves are called to be instruments of God by doing our work well in order to develop the potential inscribed by the Creator in the material world. A Christian theology of work is based on our fundamental attitudes toward the world, including both an "awe-filled contemplation of creation," represented by Francis of Assisi, and a deep respect for manual labor as spiritually meaningful, represented by Benedict of Nursia. We grow spiritually through a fruitful interplay between recollection and work, which imbues our relationship to the world with a "healthy sobriety" and deep reverence (*LS* 125–26).

According to Francis, work should be the setting for moral and spiritual growth, "where many aspects of life enter into play: creativity, planning for the future, developing our talents, living out our values, relating to others, giving glory to God" (no. 127). This theology of work is grounded in the teaching of Vatican II whereby "man is the source, the focus and the aim of all economic and social life" (*Gaudium et Spes* 63).

Employment for the Poor

Since we all have a "vocation to work" and find personal fulfillment in our work, it is important to "prioritize the goal of access to steady employment for everyone" (*LS* 127). In caring for the poor, financial assistance should always be a "provisional solution." The broader objective should always be to afford people a dignified life through work. In this regard, the pope insists that the worst material poverty is the kind that prevents people from earning a living and deprives them of the dignity of work.

Leisure

For Francis, a spirituality of work must include the proper role of rest and leisure in an integrated life that enjoys relaxation and festivity. In the United States, there is a tendency to demean rest as unproductive and unnecessary. The pope argues that this outlook undercuts the full meaning of work, which must include "a dimension of receptivity and gratuity." Rest enables us to keep our work in proper perspective so that it does not become empty activism, or foster unfettered greed, or blind us to the rights of others. Francis encourages us to keep Sunday, focused on the eucharistic celebration of the resurrection, as a day of rest that illumines the deeper meaning of our whole work week (no. 237).

For a more comprehensive papal theology of work, we have the encyclical *Laborem Exercens* of Pope John Paul II. Nevertheless, we can glean from Pope Francis some helpful insights on work, including the integral connection between respect for the material world and our responsibility to engage in meaningful work, which hones our talents and contributes to the spread of God's reign in the world.

BUSINESS

The Argentine Economy

To understand Pope Francis's perspective on business, it is important to remember that Jorge Bergoglio, ordained as a priest in 1965, carried out his ministry in his native Argentina during turbulent economic times. Until the Great Depression in the 1930s, Argentina enjoyed impressive economic development, ranking in the top ten countries in Gross Domestic Product (GDP) per capita. After 1962, the country experienced a series of economic problems, including high unemployment, chronic inflation, and a huge national debt that culminated in a national default. Bergoglio was aware of how ordinary people, especially the poor, were hurt by Argentine economic policies, typically called "crony capitalism" by critics.

Criticisms of Capitalism

The criticisms Pope Francis now levels at capitalism reflect his experience of an economic system that served the rich and exploited the poor. For example, he often cites the failures of modern neoliberal economics to serve the common good and the needs of the poor. He insists that we need to reject a "magical conception" of the market that suggests that problems can be solved simply by increasing the profits of corporations or individuals. More specifically, he criticizes "trickle down" theories that claim that economic growth, fostered by a free market, will inevitably produce greater justice and inclusion. He claims that these theories are unproven and represent "a crude and naïve trust in the goodness of those wielding economic power and in the sacralized workings of the prevailing economic system" (*Evangelii Gaudium* 54).

The Role of Government

In a letter to the 2018 meeting of the World Economic Forum in Davos, Switzerland, Francis notes that global economies, conditioned by an "ambition for profit at all costs," seem to favor fragmentation and individualism rather than more inclusive community. Recurring financial instabilities produce growing inequalities between those who enjoy a selfish opulent lifestyle and those who are reduced to "mere cogs in a machine" subject to exploitation. The pope insists that governments have a proper role to play in regulating markets, so they are more respectful of individual persons and promote family life.

Good Entrepreneurs

In his book *The Business Francis Means: Understanding the Pope's Message on the Economy*, the priest-theologian Martin Schlag claims that the interest of Francis in the world of business and his support for the "good entrepreneur who creates work," is the "unique contribution" of the pope to the social question. It is true that Francis has lauded the business world: "Business is a noble vocation, directed to producing wealth and improving our world. It can be a fruitful source of prosperity for the areas in which it operates, especially if it sees the creation of jobs as an essential part of its service to the common good" (*LS* 129). He promoted the beatification of a rich Argentine business man who administered his wealth well to help those in need to grow. Francis called true entrepreneurs "fundamental figures" in any good economy. They know their workers, sharing their fatigue and their joy of accomplishment. Recognizing the dignity of work, they avoid firing anyone if possible. The pope sharply distinguished true entrepreneurs from "speculators," who do not love their workers but see them only as "a mere means to make profit." When entrepreneurs are in charge, businesses are friends of the people and the poor. When speculators are in charge, the economy "loses its face" and people are hurt.

In his letter to the 2018 Davos participants, including President Trump, Francis also noted that entrepreneurs play an important role by "increasing the quality of productivity, creating new jobs, respecting labor laws, fighting against public and private corruption, and promoting social justice, together with the fair and equitable sharing of profits."

Summary

The Davos letter provides a balanced outline of the pope's position on business. It places his praise of enlightened business leaders in the larger context of his passionate care for the poor and marginalized persons, who suffer under current economic systems, and his conviction that the free market needs social constraints to function more justly and humanely.

CRITICS OF FRANCIS

Pope Francis, who recognizes the limitations of the Church in addressing complex social issues, has invited economic experts to respond to his major public statements, primarily *Laudato Si'*. In response, Robert Whaples, managing editor of the quarterly journal *The Independent Review*, organized a conference of generally conservative scholars on the economic views of Pope Francis. He edited the papers in a book, *Pope Francis and the Caring Society* (Independent Institute, 2017), that includes a foreword by the since-deceased Michael Novak and an introduction by Whaples himself.

Helping the Poor

Among these conservative economists, there is general agreement that Francis is excessively influenced by the crony capitalism operative in Argentina, and that he does not understand or appreciate the way free markets work in the United States. When he claims that neoliberal economies have hurt the poor, he has in mind the recent history of corruption, inflation, and unemployment in his native country and not the more moderate fluctuations in the U.S. economy. The economists say they share the pope's concern, if not his intense passion, for the billion people still living in abject poverty, but they like to remind him that worldwide poverty is not increasing, as he often says, but is rapidly declining, with two billion persons lifted above the poverty line since 1980, largely due to free-market approaches. They tend to agree with his claim that economic inequality is increasing but do not seem to share his concern that this harms the poor.

Trickle-Down Economics

One contributor, Gabriel Martinez, professor of economics at Ave Maria University, defends Francis and his criticism of trickle-down economics. Noting that Francis is not a Marxist, as some right-wing commentators claim, nor an opponent of economic liberty and rising prosperity, Martinez argues that the pope is properly concerned that this economic theory justifies indifference to the poor on the grounds that the free market will eventually take care of them. Other scholars contend that Francis does not appreciate the potential of free markets to make corrections that will benefit those on the margins. The contributors commonly dismiss the pope's strong attacks on "unfettered markets" and "unbridled capitalism" on the grounds that no existing economic system is truly free of restraints. In fact, for those conservative economists, the problem in the United States is too much regulation and not enough trust in the self-correcting dynamics of the free market.

Francis the Pastor

In this discussion, it is important to remember that Francis speaks as a pastor concerned about those left behind and not as a trained economist. Representing Christian priorities, the pope insists that we should judge free-market businesses not just on efficiency and profit but on the moral criteria of how they serve the common good and promote integral human development, especially by providing meaningful work.

CONSUMERISM

It is not easy to identify explicit critics of the challenge Pope Francis poses to consumerism, except for a few followers of Ayn Rand, who consider selfishness a virtue and advocate an opulent lifestyle. We must look deeper for possible implicit criticisms of Francis and his advocacy for a simple lifestyle. Economists argue about how to promote and sustain economic growth. On the one hand, supply-side economists stress that economies benefit more from various types of investments, such as building new plants and equipment, creating a more efficient workforce, and developing new technologies. On the other hand, Keynesian economists tend to put more emphasis on consumer buying power as exercised by the wealthy and by middle-class citizens who have a propensity to purchase durable goods, luxury items, and personal services rather than to save and invest.

Economists help us understand the dynamics of a free-market system. Consumer spending accounts for approximately 70 percent of the Gross Domestic Product (GDP). Businesses make decisions about producing and allocating goods and services based on an estimate of consumer demand. Relying on the theory that people tend to want more of the goods they like, the world of advertising uses various persuasive techniques to stimulate desire and prompt consumers to buy products. These aspects of our economy combine with other factors to create an acquisitive ethos that fosters consumerism. In other words, it is our economic system itself that functions as an implicit critic of Pope Francis. As Americans, we participate in an economic system that supports a consumerist mentality in significant ways that can escape our consciousness. It is possible to be an anonymous critic of the pope by the questionable economic decisions we make daily. It is difficult for all of us to escape completely the pervasive allure of the consumerism essential to the growth of our free-market system. By good example and prophetic word, Pope Francis challenges us to see our situation more clearly and to live gospel simplicity more fully.

The Simple Lifestyle of Francis

Pope Francis is well known for his simple lifestyle. As a priest and bishop serving in Argentina, he lived in a small apartment, cooked his own meals, and used public transportation. After his election as pope, he decided not to move into the ornate papal apartments in the Apostolic Palace but to take up residence in a three-room apartment on the second floor of the Vatican guesthouse, where he does his work, meets with people, and eats in the cafeteria. People around the globe have been touched by the simple authenticity of the first pope to take the name Francis, honoring the saint from Assisi who embraced simplicity in solidarity with the poor.

Biblical Teaching

Consistent with his lifestyle, Francis has often warned against the dangers of our consumerist culture, which promotes excessive consumption and makes an idol out of wealth and possessions. In a homily on the story of the rich man who ignored the plight of the poor man, Lazarus, in Luke (16:19–31), Francis points out that the man who enjoyed the pleasures of wealth has no name, suggesting that he lost everything that is really worthwhile for a truly fulfilling life. The rich man represents a "culture of indifference" that turns a blind eye to those banished to the margins of society. In another homily, the pope spoke of a society "intoxicated by consumerism," which celebrates hedonism and extravagances while neglecting the message of Jesus, who calls us to a simple life filled with compassion and nourished by daily prayer.

The Technocratic Paradigm

In addition to his homiletic message, Francis provides an insightful analysis of the roots and consequences of the consumerism he finds so prevalent in the United States and other developed countries. Jorge Bergoglio was greatly influenced by his never-completed doctoral studies on Romano Guardini (1885–1968), the Catholic priest-scholar who wrote *The End of the Modern World*, which is cited eight times by Pope Francis in his encyclical *Laudato Si'*. From Guardini, Francis learned the ambivalence of modern technology, which has provided cures for illness, opportunity to travel, and access to information, but has also given us great power, including the power to destroy ourselves by nuclear weapons. It has created what the pope calls a one-dimensional "technocratic paradigm" that emphasizes rational, scientific control over every aspect of life. Applied to personal relationships, it turns individuals into commodities to be controlled or used for selfish purposes. In the economic realm, this mentality tends to accept every advance in technology that increases profits without concern for its impact on human beings. Francis insists, "When money, instead of man, is at the center of the system when money becomes an idol, men and women are reduced to simple instruments of a social and economic system, which is characterized, better yet dominated, by profound inequalities. So we discard whatever is not useful" (*La Stampa*, January 11, 2015).

Radical Critiques of Consumerism

Francis urges a radical critique of consumerism and the technological paradigm from various perspectives. Morally, economic systems must be judged not just by internal factors, such as the ability to maximize profits, but by external transcendent criteria, such as serving the common good and the integral development of persons, especially the poor. Economics should be rooted in a solid anthropology that emphasizes the virtues of solidarity and the inherent dignity of all people. Christianity sets priorities that challenge consumerism: being is more important than having; cultivating virtue is more important than acquiring more material goods; and serving others is more important than satisfying every personal desire. Spiritually, Francis advocates moderating our desires, simplifying our lifestyles, and attending to the less fortunate. The pope wants us to stand back and reflect on the role technology plays in our lives, recognizing the ways it reduces our freedom and fosters an enslaving consumerism.

The Dynamics of Consumerism

In his encyclical *Laudato Si'*, which integrates care for our earth and for the poor, Pope Francis himself provides us with guidance for the reflection he recommends. In the sixth chapter, on ecological education and spirituality, the pope proposes a spirituality to counter the "competitive consumerism" fostered by the technocratic paradigm that equates freedom with being able to consume (no. 203). This paradigm, spread by globalization, creates a "collective selfishness," fosters personal greed, and promotes a "consumerist lifestyle" that leaves many people today feeling deeply dissatisfied and spiritually empty. The pope states, "The emptier a person's heart is, the more he or she needs things to buy, own and consume," creating a lifestyle that ignores the common good and the needs of others (no. 204). Reminding us that purchasing is always a moral act, the pope encourages us to reject the technocratic paradigm by simplifying our lifestyle and exercising compassionate care for our brothers and sisters (no. 206).

Cultivating Virtues

The pope recognizes that those of us who have grown up in a "milieu of extreme consumerism" will have to cultivate "sound virtues" that enable us to resist excessive consumption and be satisfied with fewer creature comforts and material goods. It is in the family setting, reinforced by the Church and educational institutions that we can best develop those virtues that lead to a "responsible simplicity of life." In the family, we learn to appreciate life, to respect nature, to use things properly, to control our greed, to express gratitude for gifts received, and "to ask without demanding" (no. 213). Francis puts special emphasis on "aesthetic education," which teaches us to "see and appreciate beauty." If we get into the habit of admiring beautiful things, we are less likely to abuse the goods of this world by excessive consumption (no. 215). The pope envisions an integrated educational effort that helps us develop the virtues needed to challenge consumerism and to enjoy a more authentic and fulfilling lifestyle.

An Ecological Spirituality

Francis proposes an "ecological spirituality," grounded on gospel teaching, which recognizes that "our vocation to be protectors of God's handiwork is essential to a life of virtue; it is not an optional or a secondary aspect of our Christian experience" (no. 217). This spirituality that involves a conversion of heart challenges "an unethical consumerism bereft of social or ecological awareness" (no. 219). In a paragraph worthy of prayerful reflection, the pope recommends a "prophetic and contemplative lifestyle, one capable of deep enjoyment free of the obsession with consumption" (no. 222). He invites us to reflect on "an ancient lesson" found in the Bible and other religious traditions: "Less is more." In our affluent society, where we are constantly bombarded by new consumer goods that can "baffle the heart," Christian spirituality advises a fulfilling alternative: "be happy with little," cherish "each moment and each thing," "stop and appreciate the small things," be "spiritually detached from what we possess," do not "succumb to sadness for what we lack," and be "serenely present" to each reality, no matter how small.

The pope argues that a moderate, simple lifestyle, freely and consciously chosen, is liberating, freeing us to live "life to the full" and to shed "unsatisfied needs." The pope insists, "Happiness means knowing how to limit some needs which only diminish us, and being open to the many different possibilities which life can offer," such as "fraternal encounters," contact with nature, service to others, enjoyment of the arts, and the practice of prayer (no. 223).

The Teaching of Christ

According to Francis, we must cultivate the virtue of humility to counter the consumerist temptation to replace God with our own ego, "enthralled with the possibility of limitless mastery over everything" (no. 224). We also need an inner peace, grounded on prayerful contemplation of the Creator God that enables us to live a "balanced lifestyle" that avoids "frenetic activity" and excessive consumption (no. 225). Jesus taught us this "attitude of the heart" when he invited us to contemplate the lilies of the field and the birds of the air. By his practice of "being present to everyone and everything," Christ "showed us the way to overcome that unhealthy anxiety which makes us superficial, aggressive and compulsive consumers" (no. 226). Francis encourages us to engage in the practice of praying before and after meals, which has many positive effects, "reminding us of our dependence on God for life," strengthening the sense of gratitude for the gifts of creation, recognizing the workers who provide us with our food, and reaffirming "our solidarity with those in greatest need" (no. 227).

Examination of Conscience

The pope's insightful analysis of the consumerism that pervades our society prompts a reflective personal examination of conscience. In what ways, perhaps subtle, am I influenced by a consumerist mentality? Does my lifestyle include any examples of excessive consumption? Do I know anything of the "spiritual emptiness" that prompts excessive buying and consumption? Do I agree with the claim that purchasing is a moral act? Can I identify any specific ways that the technocratic paradigm influences my attitudes toward wealth and possession? What virtues do I need to resist the allure of consumerism? What did I learn from my family about how to enjoy a happy, fulfilling life? Am I able to stop the busy routine of my life and enjoy the beautiful things of life? How could education help us overcome the consumerist mentality that dominates our society? What would a simpler, more contemplative lifestyle look like for me, and what concrete steps could I take to move in that direction? Do I find any practical wisdom in the Christian claim that a moderate and simple lifestyle contributes to a happier, more fulfilling, and more serene life? What inspiration do I find in reflecting on the simple, engaged lifestyle of Jesus and his teaching on overcoming anxiety by trusting God, who takes care of the birds of the air and the lilies of the field?

Pope Francis reminds us that all of our efforts to overcome consumerism and simplify our lifestyle are definitely worthwhile. "We must not think that these efforts are not going to change the world. They benefit society, often unbeknown to us, for they call forth a goodness which, albeit unseen, inevitably tends to spread" (no. 212).

CARING FOR THE POOR

Pope Francis is not an economist, nor is he interested in academic discussions of economic theories. He addresses economic issues as a pastor, serving a large transnational Church, deeply concerned that existing economic systems promote the common good and care for marginalized persons. For him, "realities are more important than ideas." He is interested in how operative economies are impacting people, especially the poor. He addresses economic issues from a moral perspective rooted in the gospel and Catholic social teaching.

Jesuits for Justice

As a Jesuit priest and bishop in Argentina, Jorge Bergoglio took seriously the commitment to serve the poor and work for justice that became a dominant theme for Jesuits under Pedro Arrupe, who served as superior general from 1965 to 1983. At their thirty-second General Congregation in 1974, the Jesuits adopted the Fourth Decree, which declared, "The Mission of the Society of Jesus today is the service of faith, of which the promotion of justice is an absolute requirement." Having personally appropriated this general theme of his religious community, especially justice for the poor, Bergoglio has consistently lived it in his various roles as parish priest, religious superior, seminary rector, archbishop of Buenos Aires, and starting in March 2013,

Bishop of Rome. In this regard, Francis has made it clear: "I feel a Jesuit in my spirituality."

Gustavo Gutiérrez

Latin American liberation theology provides another context for understanding the approach to economics espoused by Pope Francis. The seminal insight for this theological movement came from Gustavo Gutiérrez, who attempted to apply the contemporary theology he learned during his studies in Europe to his pastoral work in Lima, Peru, only to find that it did not speak to the poor people he served. That theology was designed to address people tempted to nonbelief by modern secularization. The parishioners in Lima had very different concerns. They were clearly people of faith with a strong sense of popular religiosity. Their real problem was that they were treated as nonpersons, people of no account pushed to the margins of society, treated unjustly by sinful institutions and oppressive systems. With the existential concerns of his parishioners in mind, Gutiérrez refocused on liberation themes in the Bible: the exodus, through which Yahweh granted political, social, and economic freedom to an enslaved people (see Exod 14); the prophetic message that true religion demands justice for all and care for the oppressed, including the widows, orphans, and aliens (see Isa 1:17); the claim of Jesus that he came to bring liberty to captives and to preach the good news to the poor (see Luke 4:18); and the final judgment scene in which Jesus identifies himself with the hungry, thirsty, homeless, and imprisoned (see Matt 25:31–46).

Liberation Theology

Gutiérrez and his colleagues also reinterpreted major doctrines. God is the Compassionate One who hears the cries of the poor. Christ is the liberator of those held captive. The Holy Spirit directs the works of justice by serving as our inner wellspring of spiritual energy. The Church is a servant community charged with the mission to spread the kingdom of justice and peace in the world. The Eucharist joins us to the crucified and risen Christ and strengthens us to participate in his liberating mission. Christian morality, which emphasizes the essential unity of love of God and love of neighbor, takes on a social character. It recognizes the existence of social sin, which is embedded in societal institutions and cultural patterns, producing false consciousness. It also calls us to transform social sin into liberating grace manifested in structures and institutions that serve the common good and the needs of marginalized persons. Liberation morality has an inner logic that leads to the preferential option for the poor, which calls Christians to support the poor in their efforts to become active agents of their own liberation and full participants in society. We carry out this mission with eschatological hope that one day all people will share in the abundance of the heavenly banquet.

These themes have influenced the development of Latin American liberation theology as well as other liberation theologies (black, Asian, African, feminist), which speak to people banished to the margins. Although it is true that some liberation theologians have used Marxist categories to analyze the oppressive situations of their people, the real thrust of the movement comes from refocusing scripture and retrieving liberation themes in the tradition. This leads to *orthopraxis*, that is, correct or proper action on behalf of the poor, which involves seeing their situation by experiencing it as much as possible, judging it by Christian norms, and acting collaboratively to improve it.

Theology of the People

Within the broad framework of liberation theology, there has been a movement in Latin America known as "the theology of the people," which embraces the option for the poor but with variations in methodology and points of emphasis. In his book *Pope Francis and the Theology of the People* (Orbis, 2017), Rafael Luciani gives credit to the priest-theologian Lucio Gera for providing a broad outline of a theology of the people. It starts with direct contact with "the people," a term that includes all those who belong to a specific nation as well as all the faithful, especially those who are poor. It does not use Marxist categories to analyze the oppressive situation but seeks to discern the mission of the Church based on its option for the poor. It does include both a careful study of the people's common culture to determine what is impeding the healthy development of the people as well as prudent discernment of the positive values of the people that should be preserved against the threats posed by globalization and alien ideologies. The holy faithful people, who share a common history and culture, demonstrate in their popular piety an "evangelical instinct," which promotes solidarity and rejects violence. The Church carries out its mission by evangelizing specific cultures based on an understanding of the popular religiosity or "daily mysticism" of the people.

The themes common to the theology of the people can be found in the declarations made by the Conference of Latin American Bishops (CELAM) meeting in Medellín (1968), Puebla (1979), Santo Domingo (1992), and especially Aparecida (2007), where then-Archbishop Bergoglio played an important role in drafting the concluding document. It included a chapter on the preferential option for the poor, highlighting its evangelizing and pastoral significance. It also insisted that the Church should provide Catholic professionals with ethical guidance, so they can promote economic development and higher employment rates.

Unfettered Capitalism Hurts the Poor

Drawing on his experiences as an Argentine Jesuit influenced by variations of liberation theology, Pope Francis has developed his own distinctive pastoral approach to economic issues. The pope insists, with great passion, that economic systems must do a better job of serving the cause of the poor. Although he at times acknowledges recent progress in reducing abject poverty, his passion is with those still banished to the margins. For him, the preferential option for the poor is not an abstract ideal but a moral imperative that should guide economic policies. He puts a high priority on eliminating extreme poverty in developing countries. Francis, in his apostolic exhortation *Evangelii Gaudium* (*EG*), has said, "As long as the problems of the poor are not radically resolved by rejecting the absolute autonomy of markets and financial speculation and by attacking the structural cause of inequality, no solution will be found for the world's problems or, for that matter, to any problems. Inequality is the root of social ills" (no. 202). The pope has harsh words for what he calls "unfettered capitalism," which excludes the poor and creates inequality, declaring, "Such an economy kills" (no. 53). It "tends to devour everything that stands in the way of increased profits," which renders the poor "defenseless before the interests of a deified market" (no. 56). Christians are called to give voice to "the cry of the poor," so they are not prey to the laws of an economy that treats people as mere consumers. Human rights are violated by unfair economic structures that create huge inequities.

Although Pope Francis does not offer specific solutions to the problem of poverty, his apostolic exhortation does suggest some helpful general approaches. The essential dignity of every human being, including the poor, "ought to shape all economic policies" (*EG* 203). As Christians, we are called to be "docile and attentive to the cry of the poor and to come to their aid" so that they can be "fully a part of society" (no. 187). We must be careful that the culture of prosperity does not "deaden" us, so that we become "incapable of feeling compassion at the outcry of the poor," seeing their plight as "a mere spectacle" or as "someone else's responsibility" (no. 54).

Cultivating the Virtue of Solidarity

Positively, the pope urges us to cultivate the virtue of solidarity, which recognizes deep bonds with the poor, who "have much to teach us" since, in their difficulties, they "know the suffering Christ" (EG 198). Since God gave the goods of the earth for all people, "solidarity must be lived as the decision to restore to the poor what belongs to them" (no. 189). This means "working to eliminate the structural causes of poverty" as well as providing "small daily acts of solidarity in meeting the real needs which we encounter" (no. 188). The pope encourages "financial experts and political leaders" to ponder the words of St. John Chrysostom: "Not to share one's wealth with the poor is to steal from them and to take away their livelihood. It is not our own goods which we hold, but theirs" (no. 57).

In his 2013 message for World Food Day, Francis challenges us to "educate ourselves in solidarity, to rediscover the value and meaning of this very uncomfortable word," and "to make it a basic attitude in decisions made at the political, economic and financial levels." Solidarity overcomes "selfish ways of thinking and partisan interests." It cannot be reduced to "different forms of welfare" but makes every effort "to ensure that an ever-greater number of persons are economically interdependent." For Francis, solidarity is a fundamental attitude that promotes structures, policies, and practices that enable the poor to take charge of their own lives and become active participants in the political and economic life of the community. The pope trusts that cultivating the virtue of solidarity will enable people of goodwill to develop specific concrete ways of empowering the poor.

In his encyclical *Laudato Si'*, Francis calls for a "generational solidarity" that prompts us to find comprehensive solutions and to take concrete actions to preserve the earth, our common home, for the sake of the next generation, especially the poor, who suffer the most from environmental degradation. For the pope, there is an intrinsic connection between care for the earth and care for the poor, which demands comprehensive solutions, such as the international Paris Agreement, since we cannot rely on "market forces" or "a magical conception of the market" to protect the environment so we can provide a habitable planet for future generations.

Suggesting that we can learn a "valuable lesson in solidarity" from the humble poor, Francis encourages people of affluence and power to "never tire of working for a more just world, marked by greater solidarity." In advocating for the poor, he draws on the principle of Catholic social teaching known as "the universal destination of goods," which insists that the goods of God's creation are given for the benefit of the whole human family. In a 2015 speech in Bolivia, the pope argued for a more equitable distribution of wealth on moral grounds: "Working for a just distribution of the fruits of the earth and human labor is not mere philanthropy. It is a moral obligation. For Christians, the responsibility is even greater: it is a commandment." We all bear this responsibility and must find our own distinctive ways to work for greater justice that benefits the poor.

Critics of Francis

Conservative American economists Lawrence McQuillen and Hayeon Carol Park, in their contribution to *Pope Francis and the Caring Society*, titled "Pope Francis, Capitalism, and Private Charitable Giving," argue that charitable giving is a better way of helping the poor than what they call "government redistribution" advocated by Pope Francis. They claim that state redistribution through domestic welfare programs fosters dependence and involves some type of coercion, forcing one group to share their wealth with another less fortunate group. This amounts to stealing, according to the authors, which encourages class warfare and allows "those who refuse to work" to live "off the labor of those who do work" (Oakland, CA: Independent Institute, 2017, p. 89).

Charitable Giving

In contrast, charitable giving is a free act, a voluntary transfer of goods, which fosters genuine compassion. In the United States, individuals made use of economic freedom and private property protections to build fortunes, enabling them to establish foundations (e.g., Carnegie, Ford, Rockefeller, Gates) that aid the disadvantaged. Most of the charitable giving in the United States, however, comes from individuals who give about $2,500 per household each year, totaling nearly five times as much as foundations combined. The authors contend that charitable giving is more effective than state redistribution since it promotes experimental and innovative programs to aid the poor. They argue that the redistribution advocated by Francis indirectly hurts the poor because they become dependent on government assistance.

McQuillen and Park join other economists in challenging the often-repeated statements of Francis that inequality and poverty have been rising due to globalization. They cite recent statistics showing that, from 1988 to 2011, the percentage of the world's population living in absolute poverty (incomes less than $2 per day) fell from 38 percent to 16 percent. They also reference statistics showing that a common measure of global inequality fell from 72 percent in 1988 to 67 percent in 2011. For these economists, free-market capitalism is the greatest wealth creator the world has ever seen. Their essential problem with Francis is that he does not recognize this and that his criticisms of capitalism, they say, are not only misplaced but undercut his efforts to help the poor.

Francis and Business Leaders

Pope Francis has indicated his willingness to bring greater clarity to his position on economic issues and has continued his dialogue with business leaders at major conferences. At a 2016 Fortune + Time Global Forum, he thanked a group of elite VIPs for promoting the "dignity of the human person" and for drawing attention to the plight of the poor. He urged these powerful leaders to see the human face of those in need, to listen to their stories, to give them a voice, and to learn from their experiences. He insisted that we need leaders who foster economies that promote the common good and enable all human beings to share in the resources of the world and to develop their God-given potential.

In a 2018 address to leading energy executives, Francis noted the global environmental crisis threatening the human family. He commended the executives who have adjusted their business practices in order to help protect the environment. He urged them to avoid "opportunistic and cynical efforts" to achieve short-term profits and to concentrate instead on creative long-term approaches that respect our common home and the well-being of future generations. In this address, Francis once again spoke to business leaders as a pastor and spiritual guide, imploring them to continue to use their specific talents and expertise to serve the poor and promote the good of the whole human family. Some business leaders, who sharply disagree with the pope's criticisms of unregulated free markets, remain open to his spiritual and ethical admonitions. For his part, Francis continues to promote a dialogue with leaders who have the power to shape the future. The pope offered his April 2018 prayer intention for "those who have responsibility in economic matters" that they "may have the courage to reject an economy of exclusion and know how to open new paths."

4

LITURGICAL ISSUES

DECLARATION OF POPE FRANCIS

"We can affirm with certainty and with magisterial authority that the liturgical reform is irrevocable." Pope Francis made this extremely significant declaration in the context of his address on August 24, 2017, to the participants in the sixty-eighth National Liturgical Week in Italy. For him, the reform of the liturgy set in motion by the Second Vatican Council must be allowed to proceed, undeterred by "divisive elements." Francis insists that now is not the time to rethink the Council's liturgical reforms or review the choices made in the 1963 Constitution on the Sacred Liturgy. It is time for deepening our understanding of the reform and for "internalizing" the "inspirational principles" behind it.

THE HISTORY OF LITURGICAL REFORM

The Tridentine Mass

The great significance of the pope's solemn declaration on the irreversibility of the Vatican II liturgical reform comes to light when we recall the history of modern liturgical developments. In response to the challenges of the Protestant Reformation, the Council of Trent initiated many liturgical reforms that issued in the 1570 Missal of Pius V. This liturgy, known as the Tridentine Mass, was the common form of worship for Catholics up to Vatican II and is still celebrated today. Some older Catholics can recall the role of the priest: with his back to the congregation, he led the prayers in Latin, often quietly; at the beginning he said prayers at the foot of the altar in dialogue with the boy servers who memorized the Latin responses; periodically, he turned and greeted the people; he read the epistle from the right side of the altar and, after the server moved the book, he read the gospel from the left side; on Sundays he preached a sermon in English; after saying the words of consecration, he elevated the host and chalice while the server rang the bells; he placed consecrated bread on the tongues of the people kneeling at the communion rail while rapidly repeating a prayer in Latin; he concluded the Mass by saying the last gospel, taken from the Prologue of John's Gospel.

The Vatican II liturgy includes elements not found in the Tridentine Mass: the priest facing the people; the congregation saying and singing responses; the three-year cycle of scripture readings; the prayers of the faithful; the greeting of peace; the option of receiving communion in the hand and drinking from the cup.

Early Reforms

Starting in the nineteenth century, liturgical leaders in Europe began pushing for more active participation in the liturgy, convinced that the passivity of people at Mass was contributing to the diminishment of Christian piety and witness in the world. In France, for example, Prosper Gueranger (1805–75), who restored monastic life at the Benedictine abbey of Solesmes, published a multivolume work, *The Liturgical Year*, that sparked interest in liturgical reform and eventually led to scholarly studies of the history and nature of liturgical worship.

Pope Pius X

Drawing on these developments, Pope Pius X, who served as Bishop of Rome from 1903 to 1914, described the liturgy as "the indispensable source of the Christian spirit" and encouraged reforms, including active participation and frequent communion beginning at an early age.

Virgil Michel

In the United States, Virgil Michel (1888–1938), a Benedictine monk of St. John's Abbey in Collegeville, Minnesota, played a major role in the liturgical movement that spread throughout the country. After traveling in Europe and immersing himself in liturgical developments there, Michel returned in 1925 to Collegeville and made it a center for liturgical renewal that sponsored conferences, including the National Liturgical Week starting in 1940, and published the periodical now known as *Worship*. Thanks to Michel and his numerous lectures and articles, the American version of the liturgical movement not only promoted active participation in the Eucharist but also placed a great deal of emphasis on the integral connection between liturgy and social justice.

Pope Pius XII

In 1947, Pope Pius XII made an important contribution to the liturgical movement by publishing the encyclical *Mediator Dei*, which established a sound theological basis for reforming the liturgy and promoting active participation in the Eucharist.

He also made a practical contribution to the movement by restoring the Easter Vigil.

THE CONSTITUTION
ON THE SACRED LITURGY

In his 2017 Liturgical Week Address, Pope Francis referred to the liturgical movement as an initial response to "the discomfiture perceived in ecclesial prayer." It bore fruit in the Second Vatican Council and its Constitution on the Sacred Liturgy (*Sacrosanctum Concilium*), which responded to "real needs and to the concrete hope of renewal." The Constitution, the first of the sixteen documents produced by the Council, passed with only three dissenting votes and was promulgated on December 4, 1963. Francis, who did not participate in Vatican II, views the document as expressing "in a renewed way the perennial vitality of the Church in prayer" while maintaining "the principle of respect for healthy tradition and legitimate progress."

General Principles

The first chapter of the Constitution presents general principles to guide the reform of the liturgy. Christ is present at Mass in various ways: in the consecrated bread and wine; in the scriptural word; in the person of the presider; and in the assembly of the faithful (*Sacrosanctum Concilium* 7). Liturgy is the "exercise of the priestly office of Jesus Christ," the full public worship "performed by the Mystical Body of Jesus Christ," and a "sacred action surpassing all others" (no. 7). It is "the summit toward which the activity of the Church is directed" and "the fount from which all her power flows" (no. 10). The faithful are called to "full, conscious, and active participation in liturgical celebrations" (no. 14).

Liturgical Issues

The reform of the liturgy should be guided by certain norms. The rites should be characterized by "a noble simplicity." They should be "short, clear, and free from useless repetitions" so that the people can comprehend them without much explanation (no. 34). Since "scripture is of the greatest importance in the celebration of the liturgy," it is essential to cultivate a "warm and lively appreciation" of the biblical word (no. 24) and to restore a "more ample, more varied and more suitable reading from sacred scripture" for liturgical celebrations (no. 35). The Council allowed the use of vernacular languages in the liturgy and gave "the competent territorial ecclesiastical authority," for example, bishops' conferences (no. 22), the power to make decisions, subject to confirmation by the Apostolic See, about the use of the vernacular and proper translations from the Latin (no. 36). The precise wording and intended meaning of this directive has become a major source of friction between Francis and his curial critics.

Active Participation

The second chapter of the Constitution contains several decrees promoting full and conscious participation in the liturgy so the faithful are not at Mass "as strangers or silent spectators" (no. 48). The rites are to be simplified, with duplications and unnecessary additions omitted, and useful elements from the early Church restored (no. 50). "The treasures of the Bible are to be opened up more lavishly" so that over a number of years the faithful attending Mass will hear a "more representative part of the sacred scriptures" (no. 51). The Council put greater emphasis on the homily, which is an integral part of the eucharistic liturgy and should be based on the scripture readings (no. 52). It also allowed the practice of the laity receiving the consecrated wine at Mass (no. 55) and expanded the opportunities for concelebration, which manifests the "unity of the priesthood" (no. 57).

Other Sacraments

In chapter 3, on the other sacraments, the bishops introduced some changes worth noting: revising the rite of confirmation so that it appears more clearly as part of Christian initiation; changing the name of "extreme unction" to "anointing of the sick" to indicate it is for anyone in danger of death from sickness or old age; and restoring the adult catechumenate.

Implementation

When Pope Francis declared that the liturgical reform is irreversible, he was referring to the renewal officially set in motion by the Constitution on the Sacred Liturgy, passed overwhelmingly by the Second Vatican Council, and gradually implemented over the next decades. Of special note were the first Masses in English in the United States on the First Sunday of Advent on November 29, 1964, and the publication of the new Missal in 1970.

Francis felt the need to make his authoritative declaration because some Catholics, clerical and lay, have continued to resist various elements of the reform. Early opposition was led by French Archbishop Marcel Lefebvre (1905–91), who participated in Vatican II but refused to support some of the documents. His vigorous opposition to the Council, including the liturgical changes, led to his suspension in 1976 and his excommunication in 1988. Some of his followers returned to communion with Rome, but others, the Society of St. Pius X, have continued their opposition. At a popular level, the traditionalist Catholic group *Rorate Coeli* continues to recruit priests to offer the Tridentine Mass for the poor souls in purgatory, claiming that as many as seventy-six American priests do so regularly.

Out of concern for elderly priests, Pope Paul VI allowed the celebration of the Tridentine Mass in certain circumstances. In 2007, Pope Benedict issued *Summorum Pontificum*, expanding permission for all priests to celebrate in private the 1962 Tridentine Mass, called the "extraordinary form" of the one Roman Rite. This presented the possibility of priests using this form with a congregation and even doing so at a regular parish liturgy. Traditionalists have used this option to multiply opportunities to attend Latin Masses.

Reform of the Reform

In his 1997 memoir, *Milestones*, Cardinal Joseph Ratzinger called for a "new liturgical movement," which came to be called a "reform of the reform," to correct the harmful liturgical errors and distortions caused by emphasizing the discontinuity between Vatican II and the living tradition of the Church. Cardinal Ratzinger insisted the Church urgently needed "a liturgical reconciliation" that recognizes the unity of the history of the liturgy and understands Vatican II not as a break from the past but as a stage of development. After his election as pope, Benedict delivered an address to the Roman Curia that blamed the "hermeneutic of discontinuity" (interpretations of Vatican II that emphasize the differences between the Tridentine and Vatican II liturgies) for creating more subjective approaches to the liturgy that neglect its divine origin and goal. The "reform of the reform" movement and the great availability of the 1962 Latin Mass, authorized by Pope Benedict, helped energize opposition to the Vatican II liturgical reform that prompted the strong defense of the Council by Pope Francis.

Translations of the Latin Liturgy

The important task of producing English translations of the original Latin liturgical texts has generated a great deal of controversy. Sensing a need for an improved translation, the International Committee for English in the Liturgy (ICEL), composed of representatives of eleven English-speaking countries, gathered a group of experts in the early 1980s, who worked for seventeen years to produce a new translation. In 1998, ICEL presented to the Vatican what many considered a fine version of the Sacramentary only to have it totally rejected, even though Vatican II had given regional conferences of bishops the authority to produce translations. Furthermore, in 2001, Rome promulgated *Liturgiam Authenticum*, which demanded more literal translations of the Latin texts with nothing added and nothing omitted. The Vatican then produced its own English translation, which was implemented in 2011.

Dissatisfaction with the English Translation

Since 2011, polls indicate most Catholics, clergy and laity, do not like the translation, finding it wooden, stilted, ungrammatical, and, at times, unintelligible. Theologically, it places more emphasis on God's transcendence than divine imminence, more on merit than mercy. Many of the prayers are one sentence long with multiple clauses, making it difficult to understand for presiders reading them, let alone parishioners hearing them. Those who long for a more intelligible and aesthetic prayer experience at Mass can find some hope in two recent decisions of Pope Francis. He is supporting a commission to do a critical study of *Liturgiam Authenticum*, which provided the theoretical basis for the current literal translation. He also issued the statement *Magnum Principium*, which reendorsed Vatican II's directive that national hierarchies oversee translating liturgical texts. Thus, we see that disputes over translations also contributed to the pope's strong affirmation of the reform fostered by the Council.

Cardinal Sarah

Cardinal Robert Sarah, former archbishop of Conakry, Guinea, and current influential prefect of the Congregation of

Liturgical Issues

Divine Worship (CDW), has emerged as an unofficial leader of the reform of the reform movement, at times putting him at odds with Pope Francis, who appointed him to his current position. Sarah made his criticisms of the Vatican II liturgy public in his book *The Power of Silence: The Dictatorship of Noise,* which includes an afterword by former Pope Benedict, who wrote that the "liturgy was in good hands" with the man he had named a cardinal and recommended as the prefect of CDW. Sarah has encouraged priests presiding at Mass to face east with their back to the assembly, which drew a public rebuke from Francis. He has also disparaged the ancient tradition and current practice of receiving communion in the hand while standing, suggesting it is the work of Satan and shows a lack of submission to God. In response to the pope's *Magnum Principium,* which reaffirmed the authority of national conferences of bishops over liturgical translations, Sarah published an article claiming his Congregation still had control over translations as a parent over a child or a professor over a student. In this article, which was widely distributed throughout Europe and the United States, the cardinal also insisted that the literal translation rules were still in place. Francis responded with a letter clarifying the intent of *Magnum Principium,* insisting that liturgical translations no longer must conform in all points to the norms of *Liturgiam Authenticum,* as was previously the case. The responsibility to translate faithfully now belongs to episcopal conferences and not to the Congregation for Divine Worship, whose confirmation responsibility "no longer supposes a detailed word-by-word examination." The Congregation should not impose on episcopal conferences a translation it produced, as "this would undermine the right of the bishops sanctioned…by *Sacrosanctum Concilium.*" Finally, Francis asked Sarah to share his clarifying letter with the bishops, the members of his Congregation, and the media outlets.

The Altar

In his address to the Italian liturgists on August 24, 2017, Francis devoted a paragraph to the altar as a sign of Christ, "the cornerstone of the spiritual building," where worship is offered to the living God in spirit and truth. The altar, which we venerate, is "the center toward which our churches focus attention" and the place from which we are nourished by "the bread of life and the cup of salvation." Thus, the pope provides a solid theological reason for maintaining the present postures at Mass that undercuts the arguments for facing east.

Liturgy as a Fount of Life

It is possible to read the rest of the pope's address to Italian liturgists as a reflection on the Constitution on the Sacred Liturgy of Vatican II. Francis insists that the liturgy is "popular" and not clerical. It is an action of God himself for our benefit, but also the action of the people who listen to God and respond in prayer. The liturgical assembly is inclusive, overcoming "in Christ every boundary of age, race, language and nation." Liturgical worship "is not primarily a doctrine to be understood, or a rite to be performed." Rather, "it is a fount of life and of light for our pilgrimage of faith."

By his authoritative declaration that the Vatican II renewal is irreversible, Pope Francis has rejected the reform of the reform movement, a phrase he dislikes and calls "an error." This means there is no reason for a dialogue between those who accept the directives of the Council and those who favor the Tridentine Mass, which is itself "an exception" to the ordinary liturgical life of the Church. National hierarchies know best how to judge vernacular translations. Presiders should face the altar and not the east. The Vatican II liturgy, properly understood, is not inherently too subjective since it is the work of God and of the people.

Liturgical Issues

There is no room for clericalism in the liturgy, which must be popular and inclusive.

Pope Francis has spoken with decisive authority and great pastoral care. Those of us who support him can hope that his initiative will prove to be a significant moment in the ongoing effort to revitalize the liturgy as the fount of Christian life.

5

DIVORCE AND REMARRIAGE ISSUES

THE JOY OF LOVE

"Love in Marriage"

The apostolic exhortation *Amoris Laetitia* (*The Joy of Love*), officially issued by Pope Francis on the Feast of St. Joseph, March 19, 2016, is a rich resource for constructive reflection on contemporary marriage and family life. For example, the fourth chapter, "Love in Marriage," includes a collection of scripture quotations that illumine the nature and function of family life; a realistic assessment of cultural trends that challenge Christian ideals; a summary of Church teaching; and helpful suggestions for a spirituality of marriage and married love.

In that chapter, Francis describes marriage as "the icon" of God's love for us, which makes of the "two spouses one single existence" (no. 121). The grace of the sacrament enriches the love between husband and wife, combining "the warmth of friendship and erotic passion" in an "affective union" that "endures long after emotions and passions subside" (no. 120). No married couple achieves all these marital ideals. No marriage is a perfect reflection of God's love for humanity or Christ's love for the Church. No family is totally effective in passing on Christian teachings and values.

Chapter 8

Media attention, however, focused more on controversial issues, especially communion for divorced and remarried Catholics. Pope Francis takes up that issue in a very subtle and sometimes ambiguous eighth chapter, which deals with marriages that fall short of the Christian ideal. The pope describes the ideal in this way:

> Christian marriage, as a reflection of the union between Christ and his Church, is fully realized in the union between a man and a woman who give themselves to each other in a free, faithful and exclusive love, who belong to each other until death and are open to the transmission of life, and are consecrated by the sacrament, which grants them the grace to become a domestic church and a leaven of new life for society. (no. 292)

Crucially, the pope sees less-than-perfect marriages not as sinful but as partial embodiments of an ideal that are open to further development.

NEW TESTAMENT IDEALS

Theologians and scripture scholars have taught us to see the New Testament as an eschatological document that proposes ideals that will never be completely achieved in this life but only in the next life of heaven. The kingdom is already here but is not yet complete. There are signs of God's reign in the world today, but the final triumph of divine grace awaits the Parousia, the completion of Christ's saving work. Recognizing gospel mandates as eschatological ideals protects us against a self-righteous attitude that we are perfect, while prompting us to strive diligently to move toward the ideal. The Church's task is to help us make progress on that journey.

FOLLOWING THE EXAMPLE OF CHRIST

Pope Francis has demonstrated his pastoral genius by placing his whole discussion of marriage within that eschatological framework of gospel ideals. While recognizing that some unions contradict the ideal, Francis insists that others "realize it in at least a partial and analogous way." The pastoral task is to discern, name, and develop the grace already at work in partial ways. The pope encourages us to follow the example of Christ, who gazed with love on frail human beings, who patiently guided the Samaritan woman to "the full joy of the Gospel," and who taught us not to cast off people but to follow "the way of mercy and reinstatement," which reaches out and welcomes all those in need. The Church should function like "a field hospital," caring for the weakest who are wounded in the battles of life. The pastoral art is to help couples discern the next step they can take to move toward the Christian ideal of marriage.

PASTORAL GUIDANCE

Applying the "law of gradualness" proposed by Pope John Paul II, Francis recognizes that couples advance spiritually "by different stages of growth" as they gradually integrate the gifts of divine love and "the demands of God's definitive and absolute love." Pastors should dialogue with couples to discover "elements in their lives that can lead to a greater openness to the Gospel of marriage in its fullness." There is a "divine pedagogy of grace" leading couples to "reach the fullness of God's plan for them."

Francis applies this general pastoral approach to various "irregular situations" that fall short of the ideal. In examining "simple cohabitation," unmarried couples living together, the pope distinguishes those who are opposed to anything institutional or definite, which is a source of concern, from those who delay marriage for economic reasons, such as the lack of a job or steady income as well as the high cost of a wedding in some countries. While recognizing that some unions "radically contradict" gospel ideals, the pope notes that others are characterized by deep affection and the ability to overcome trials, "signs of love which in some way reflect God's own love." Without citing any data, Francis claims that an increasing number of couples living together request marriage in the Church. Pastors should welcome all such couples, guiding them "patiently and discreetly" to "the full reality of marriage and family in conformity with the Gospel."

DIVORCE SITUATIONS

Turning to divorced and remarried Catholics, Francis recognizes various situations that defy rigid classifications and call for "a suitable personal and pastoral discernment." Some second marriages have been "consolidated over time," with "new children, proven fidelity, generous self-giving, Christian commitment." Some individuals were unjustly abandoned in their first marriage or entered a second marriage for the sake of the children. Others are "subjectively certain in conscience that their previous and irreparably broken marriage had never been valid."

NO NEW GENERAL RULES

Given the great variety of concrete situations, Francis makes this important statement: "It is understandable that neither the

Synod nor this Exhortation could be expected to provide a new set of general rules, canonical in nature and applicable to all cases." There are no "easy recipes" to apply to diverse situations. Instead, the pope encourages "a pastoral discernment of particular cases," which recognizes that, since there are various degrees of responsibility, "the consequences or effects of a rule need not necessarily always be the same." As Aquinas taught, general rules identify a good that must be upheld, but the application in specific situations may vary.

DISCERNMENT

Francis offers helpful pastoral advice on the process of discernment. The divorced and remarried should do an examination of conscience, asking themselves pertinent questions: How did they treat the children during the divorce process? Did they seek reconciliation when the marriage was in trouble? What has become of their former spouse? How has their new relationship affected the rest of the family and the community? What example is being set for young people preparing for marriage?

INTERNAL FORUM

The pope encourages the use of what is traditionally known as "the internal forum," which involves remarried couples having a serious conversation together with their pastor to discern concrete steps toward fuller participation in the life of the Church. This discernment process should always respect the "Gospel demands of truth and charity" and never give the impression that exceptions to the general rules can be easily attained or that the Church maintains a double standard. It is a dynamic process that should help form "an enlightened conscience" that can recognize "the most generous response that can be given to God" in the "concrete complexity" of a person's limited situation.

POPE FRANCIS AND HIS CRITICS

WELCOMING THE REMARRIED

Following the majority of synod fathers, Francis wants divorced and remarried Catholics to be more fully integrated into Christian communities while avoiding scandal. "They are baptized; they are brothers and sisters; and the Holy Spirit pours into their hearts gifts and talents for the good of all" (no. 299). Pastors should treat them not as excommunicated persons but as living members of the Church "who deserve welcome and encouragement" along the path of life and the Gospel. "It can no longer be simply said that all those in any irregular situation are living in a state of mortal sin and are deprived of sanctifying grace." There may well be "mitigating factors" that limit the culpability of persons in irregular marriages; for example, affective immaturity or the force of acquired habit, as noted in the *Catechism of the Catholic Church*. Given these factors, pastors should not simply apply moral laws to the divorced and remarried "as if they were stones to throw at people's lives." Rather, they should enter a process of discernment that helps couples find "possible ways of responding to God and growing" in "the life of grace and charity, while receiving the Church's help to this end." At this point, Pope Francis adds the extremely significant footnote, note 351, which states, "In certain cases this can include the help of the sacraments." Specifying the point, he reminds us that the confessional is not a "torture chamber" but rather "an encounter with the Lord's mercy," and that the Eucharist is "not a prize for the perfect, but a powerful medicine and nourishment for the weak."

THE FULL IDEAL OF MARRIAGE

Lest he be misunderstood, Francis insists that dealing mercifully with irregular marriages does not undercut the Church's proclamation of "the full ideal of marriage, God's plan in all its grandeur." The pope states, "To show understanding in the face of exceptional situations never implies dimming the light of the fuller ideal, or proposing less than what Jesus offers to the human being."

ADVICE TO PASTORS

With that clarification, Francis once again reminds pastors to accompany with mercy and patience couples called to take steps toward the ideal of Christian marriage, treating them with compassion while avoiding harsh judgement. The pope knows some "prefer a more rigorous pastoral care which leaves no room for confusion." He believes, however, that Jesus wants pastors to engage in the complex reality of people's lives, bringing "the balm of mercy" and "the power of tenderness." When pastors leave their comfortable niches and meet people where they really are, their lives become "wonderfully complicated."

Pope Francis concludes the eighth chapter by encouraging those in "complicated situations" to speak with their pastors or committed laypersons, searching for some light on the path to personal growth and their proper place in the Church.

REACTIONS TO THE POPE'S TEACHING

Reactions to the pope's approach to communion for divorced and remarried Catholics have varied greatly. Those who wanted clear rules either allowing or forbidding communion have expressed disappointment that he refused to take a stand. Several commentators pointed out that only a relatively small number of Catholics see it as a personal concern, since most divorced and remarried have either left the Church or go to communion despite current rules. *Boston Globe* columnist James Carroll, a former priest, argued that Francis all but explicitly opened communion to the divorced and remarried and lauded him for bringing into the light the long-standing secretive practice of the "internal forum." As Carroll recalled from his own days as a priest, couples typically talked to their pastors and prayerfully made their own decision about communion.

Cardinal Raymond Burke, who was born in 1948, educated in Rome, and served as archbishop of St. Louis from 2004 to 2008, has emerged as the major clerical critic of chapter 8 of *Amoris Laetitia*. Burke, who served in the Vatican Curia as prefect of the Apostolic Tribunal from 2008 to 2014, has been generally critical of Pope Francis, claiming that the Church under his leadership is like a ship without a rudder. In November 2016, Burke, along with three other retired cardinals, sent a *Dubia*, a series of five questions, to Francis asking for clear answers on communion for divorced and remarried Catholics. The implication of their questions is that the pope has gone against the traditional Catholic position on the indissolubility of a sacramental marriage. When Francis refused to answer the questions, Burke threatened the pope with "a formal act of correction." Some American bishops share Burke's concerns. For example, Archbishop Charles Chaput of Philadelphia issued guidelines for his diocese that close off any possibility of divorced and remarried Catholics receiving communion without an annulment of prior marriages.

ROSS DOUTHAT

The *New York Times* columnist Ross Douthat, a self-identified conservative Catholic, initially suggested that conservatives do not know how to respond to a document that "if read straightforwardly seems to introduce various kinds of ambiguity into the church's official teaching on marriage, sin and the sacraments," which provide "theological cover" for those in favor of a path to reconciliation and communion. Douthat identified some possible conservative responses: declare victory because the exhortation did not change doctrine; read it in light of previous Church teaching and argue there is "no rupture" and "everything is fine"; question the authority of the document, which is an exhortation and does not carry the same weight as an encyclical; and his own approach, which acknowledges the ambiguities in the text even though this opens the door to more liberal interpretations. As we noted in chapter 1, Douthat's book *To Change the Church* goes further, arguing that the efforts of Francis to soften the Church's consistent teaching on the indissolubility of marriage risks breaking faith with Christ, threatens to divide the Church, and opens up the possibility of schism. Since the book attempts to establish a grand narrative to support its radical claims, it is necessary to summarize the major points in the book, focusing on the author's own words and ideas, before proposing important critiques.

Interpretations of Vatican II

Douthat begins by comparing liberal and conservative interpretations of Vatican II, both of which failed to achieve the goal of the revitalization of the Church envisioned by Pope John XXIII in calling the Council. The liberal project, which embraced the spirit of Vatican II, centered on the fundamental shift from a vertical conception of the Church as a hierarchical institution to a horizontal view of the Church as the people of God. After the Council, the liberal dream of progress was thwarted by *Humanae Vitae*, forbidding artificial birth control, and by the conservative papacies of John Paul II and Benedict XVI, lasting a total of thirty-five years. This liberal project not only failed to energize the Church but, according to Douthat, also caused numerical losses in Mass attendance and religious vocations.

The conservative project, led by John Paul and his successor, Benedict, insisted that Vatican II maintained continuity with previous Church teaching. The conservatives were critical of the excesses of liberals during the 1970s, insisting that a careful reading of the actual Vatican II documents in no way justified such innovations in Church doctrine and practice. Although some conservative institutions did better numerically, and conservative bishops and cardinals outnumbered the liberals, Douthat contends that the conservative project was not able to meet the challenges of the Church in the modern world. By 2013, when Pope Benedict resigned, conservatives and liberals were living in an uneasy truce, which left the Church intact but too weak to be the revitalized force for good envisioned by the Council fathers.

The Election of Francis

According to Douthat, Jorge Bergoglio was elected Bishop of Rome on March 13, 2013, because the liberal cardinals, led by Walter Kasper, liked his stated desire for the Church to engage the contemporary world by going out to the peripheries and because enough conservative cardinals saw him as continuing the "new evangelization" of John Paul. Bergoglio's choice of the name "Francis," after the saint from Assisi, signaled his care for the poor and his intention to continue to live a simple lifestyle. During his first year, Francis created a public image of the people's pope dedicated to reform. He did this by symbolic gestures (washing the feet of a young Muslim girl), appointments of pastoral bishops (Blaise Cupich as archbishop of Chicago), and informal comments ("Who am I to judge?"). Douthat summarized this development: "There could be no real doubt, a year or more into his pontificate, that the new pontiff saw his papacy as a corrective to the John Paul and Benedict years." He intended "a more experimental and adventuresome papal style, a less rigorous approach to public teaching on faith and morals," and greater engagement with the modern world. The positive response to Francis indicated that the Catholic Church, despite scandals and mismanagement, could still make a difference in the modern world.

The Synods on the Family

For Douthat, it all started to break down when Francis called a synod on the vocation and mission of the family, held in two parts: the "extraordinary" synod of 2014 to set the agenda and the 2015 "ordinary" synod to discuss the major issues. He goes into detail on the ongoing clash between liberals, led by Cardinal Kasper, who wanted to provide a path to full communion for the divorced and remarried, and the conservatives, led by Cardinal Burke, who argued that this would undercut the traditional teaching on the indissolubility of a sacramental marriage. Douthat portrays Francis as repeatedly using his power to support the liberal position by his daily homilies, his remarks to the media, and his appointment of progressives to key positions, especially those charged with drafting the final report. Through last-minute negotiations in the German-language group, the liberals came to an agreement with Gerhard Müller, the conservative prefect of the Congregation for the Doctrine of the Faith, on a statement that read, "Conversation with the priest, in the internal forum, contributes to the formation of a correct judgment on what hinders the possibility of a fuller participation in the life of Christ and Church practices." The statement went on with this caveat: "This discernment can never prescind from the Gospel demands of truth and charity as proposed by the Church." Liberals claimed this opened the door to the Kasper proposal, while conservatives argued that the traditional teaching was still in place. Douthat portrayed Francis as angry in defeat: "His two-year synodal project, stage-managed to build a Vatican II–esque consensus behind a major, headline-capturing reform, had ended with the pontiff on the losing side of precisely the processes that he had championed." Not only that, but in the process, the pope, elected to move the Church beyond internal civil war, "had turned bishops against bishops, theologians against theologians and raised the stakes in the church's internal conflict to their highest point in decades" (p. 125).

Amoris Laetitia

Five months after the synod ended, Francis published *Amoris Laetitia*, which, according to Douthat, "yearned in the direction of changing the church's rules for communion," fueled by a logic that such a change is reasonable and desirable. Yet the pope "never said so directly, never made explicit what he repeatedly implied." The text did encourage pastors to accompany couples in irregular marriages, helping them to "grow in the life of grace and charity." As noted above, footnote 351 added, "In certain cases, this can include the help of the sacraments." Again, Douthat sees this footnote as deliberately unclear, leaving open various interpretations. In the United States, some bishops, for example, Archbishop Charles Chaput, have stated clearly that the traditional teaching and practice is still in place and must be followed. Others, including Bishop Robert McElroy of San Diego, are open to individuals, assisted by their pastors, prayerfully deciding to receive communion. Most of the world's approximately five thousand bishops have, however, "declined to take a firm stand," waiting to see how things develop. Douthat suggests that the pope's strategy is to buy time so that the consensus he had failed to win at the synod "could gradually emerge" and the whole Catholic world be united on treating the remarried with mercy.

Argentine Bishops

For his part, Francis wrote a private letter to the Argentine bishops praising them for their guidelines that effectively opened the possibility of some remarried and divorced persons to receiving communion. His letter included the statement that "no other interpretations" were possible. In this regard, it is significant that the conservative former prefect of CDF, Cardinal Gerhard Müller, in an interview with the *National Catholic Register*, defended the orthodoxy not only of *Amoris* on communion but also of the Argentine guidelines interpreting and applying this teaching.

Douthat also criticizes the pope for not responding to the "reasonable" questions posed by Cardinal Burke and others in their *Dubia*, even after they made it public. "So the *Dubia*, no less than *Amoris* itself, hung there unanswered and unresolved."

The Liberal Project

Given this confusing situation, Douthat explores various paths forward. He admits that to this point the tension exists primarily among "professional Catholics," clerics, theologians, and journalists, with no "grassroots rebellion brewing." Among the liberal elites, he detects a desire for more radical changes, such as intercommunion with Protestants and recognizing gay marriage. He recalls the history of the Arian heresy in the fourth century when faithful believers, led by St. Athanasius, held true to orthodox Church teaching, while many bishops and possibly Pope Liberius, did not. Perhaps there could be an unlikely conservative victory in a future council that preserves orthodoxy but prompts some liberals to break away and form their own new church. He also considers an unwelcomed liberal victory that involves further accommodations to the modern secular world and leaves conservatives with various bad options; giving in to the liberals, enduring as a beleaguered faction within the Church, and going into schism like the Society of St. Pius X. For Douthat, however, the liberal teaching on communion is antigospel, against the clear teaching of Jesus as found in Mark's Gospel, a break with traditional teaching, and a betrayal of the many who sacrificed to be faithful to the clear teaching of the Church. There is no higher morality that can relativize the absolute moral obligations proclaimed by Christ. If the liberal position prevails, the Catholic Church will go the way of the Anglican Communion that is divided and weakened.

The Conservative Project

In assessing the legacy of Pope Francis, Douthat notes many factors limiting the success of his liberal project. There is little evidence that his approach is bringing back lapsed Catholics, increasing Mass attendance, or inspiring new vocations. The younger Catholic priests are more conservative than their older colleagues. There are strong conservative movements in France and especially in Africa with its rapidly growing Catholic population. Many conservative bureaucrats remain in the Vatican Curia. In the political realm, the neoliberal consensus is under attack by various forms of populism, including that of President Trump. Just as it is hard to see how conservatives can successfully resist the liberalizing project of Francis, it is also difficult to envision a total progressive victory, given all the conservative factors at work in global Catholicism.

Douthat Summary

In his summary analysis, Douthat laments that the great promise of Francis's pontificate has been blunted by his position on communion for the remarried. Unfortunately, the pope has turned against his conservative critics, dismissing them as legalists and ignoring the "cultural-political fears" of Catholics attracted to "right-wing nationalists," including Donald Trump. Douthat goes further: "Francis has not just exposed conflicts; he has stoked them, encouraging sweeping ambitions among his allies and apocalyptic fears among his critics." In the process, he has undercut the quest for common ground and pushed the Church to the edge of schism with no clear unifying resolution.

Positive Reviews of *To Change the Church*

The secular world is disposed to accept Douthat's grand narrative. For example, an article in *National Review* by Alexander Desanctis calls Douthat's book "a successful, engaging and well written portrait of Pope Francis" that offers "a compelling blend of history and theology to analyze the Church's internal divisions in recent decades, skillfully examining how Francis's agenda and personality might alter the Church's course, perhaps even for generations to come."

The conservative magazine *The Weekly Standard* published a lengthy review by Stephen White claiming that Douthat, a "thoughtful and pious" critic, "has written the most balanced and least polemical of the recent critiques of this pontificate." Even in a mostly critical *New York Times* review of *To Change the Church*, Georgetown scholar Paul Elie admits that Douthat provides "an adroit, perceptive, gripping account" of the liberal and conservative "master narratives" interpreting Vatican II and offers "a third narrative that deftly blends the two." Given the potential influence of *To Change the Church*, supporters of Francis need to challenge some of the major points in its narrative.

Critical Reviews

Journalist Michael Sean Winters published in the *National Catholic Reporter* a devastating review, claiming Douthat's "facts are nonsense, his arguments tendentious, and his thesis shockingly absurd." Quoting substantial passages from the book characterizing the 2015 synod, Winters asked three bishops who attended the synod to comment on Douthat's portrayals. In each case, the bishops indicated Douthat either had the facts wrong or misinterpreted the dynamics of the synod. For example, Douthat claimed the mood in Rome at the close of the synod was "paranoid and toxic" and the mood among the hierarchy "distrustful and disappointed." One bishop said this was "absolutely not correct," adding that every paragraph of the final document received, by secret ballot, a minimum of two-thirds support and most close to unanimous approval.

Winters also accused Douthat of having an uninformed understanding of Catholic theology that reduces it to "the binary simplicity" of liberals versus conservatives while failing to appreciate its historical development. Finally, Winters attacks Douthat for his "grotesque" comparison of Pope Francis to Donald Trump, insisting that Francis is not a "vulgar, misogynistic narcissist with little learning and a short attention span." For Winters, *To Change the Church* is a "disgrace," wrong on facts, wrong on theology, and wrong on Pope Francis.

In a less harsh, but still critical, review published in the April 2, 2018, issue of *America* magazine, theologian Thomas Rausch first praises Ross Douthat as an "astute, often insightful Vaticanologist" and summarizes, without criticism, his narrative of the election of Jorge Bergoglio, his promising early years as Pope Francis, and his calling of the synod on family life that brought the Church to the edge of schism. However, he then notes that Douthat's argument "frequently overreaches," pointing out that while the Church has always honored the teaching of Jesus on divorce and remarriage, it has often made "pastoral accommodations," allowing remarriage. For example, the Apostle Paul allowed Christians to remarry if their unbelieving spouses separated from them, and the Eastern Orthodox have maintained to this day the possibility of divorced persons getting married in the Church. Rausch claims Douthat "most falls short" in his understanding of the Church, describing it not as a spiritual community but as "a political body of bishops," constantly juxtaposing "liberals and conservatives, progressive factions and traditionalist cardinals." *To Change the Church* ignores the pope's efforts "to respect synodality in a global church" and his emphasis on "the place of conscience and discernment in the church's life." On the issue of reception of the teaching of *Amoris Laetitia*, Rausch notes 62 percent of Catholics favor allowing communion for the divorced and remarried, and that Douthat himself "admits the resistance to Francis is small, more a battle among elites than with the grassroots of Catholicism." The implication seems to be that the real situation does not point to the schism feared by Douthat.

Paul Baumann, editor of *Commonweal*, argues that Douthat's reading of Christ's prohibition of divorce (see Mark 10:9) does not consider historical developments. Just decades after Mark, the evangelist Matthew granted an exception for unchastity (see Matt 5:32). The Pauline privilege allows Catholics in failed marriages to unbaptized spouses to marry again in the Church. Baumann argues that history challenges Douthat's notion that the Church has always defended the indissolubility of marriage without exception. Furthermore, "there has been more diversity and discontinuity in the development of doctrine than Douthat is willing to allow." He claims the Church teaching can develop but cannot be "revised, contradicted and transcended," even though it seems evident that Vatican II did precisely this in the case of religious liberty. Although Douthat recognizes that the Church in times of crisis "has again and again found renewal from below," he is unwilling to consider that the efforts of Pope Francis to decentralize Church authority is designed to make space precisely for that renewal from below. Baumann concludes by suggesting that Douthat's dire predictions of chaos in the Church is not the only possibility. By offering pastoral guidance to divorced and remarried Catholics, Pope Francis has opened the possibility of making the Church's wisdom on marriage and sexuality credible again.

THEOLOGICAL CRITICISMS

My own fundamental criticism of Douthat, who makes no claims to theological expertise, is that he presumes a simplistic view of divine grace, without recognizing how this influences his grand narrative. A contemporary theology of grace affirms that the Holy Spirit is at work in the whole of human history and in the Church, which names this divine activity. This means that the secular world, always a mixture of sin and grace, at times achieves and manifests truth, goodness, and beauty. Although liberal modernity has generated excessive individualism, sexual license, and selfish consumerism, it has also fostered human rights, political democracy, and economic progress.

Development of Doctrine

At the same time, the Church, which is the official guardian and expositor of the revelation manifested most completely in Jesus Christ, as witnessed in the normative scriptures, is always in process of achieving a deeper understanding of that revelation without ever totally comprehending or perfectly expressing it. Historically, the Church only gradually came to see that slavery violated the fundamental teaching of Jesus on love of neighbor and that the right of all persons to religious liberty is indeed in accord with his respect for personal freedom. From the perspective of this theology of grace and revelation, history cannot be reduced to a struggle between an evil secular world and a Church equipped with a complete and unchanging deposit of truths, as Douthat claims. There is, rather, an ongoing dialogue between specific historical and cultural developments, which are always a mix of grace and sin, and the Church, which draws on gospel wisdom to affirm and criticize these developments. In this dialogue, each side can learn from the other and both can move toward a deeper appropriation of divine truth. For Christians participating in the dialogue, the cross remains judge of the flag, Christ deserves our allegiance before the country, the gospel provides a higher perspective than nationalism, and the teachings of the Church, proposed infallibly in dogmas and authoritatively in doctrines, supersedes cultural and societal standards. These definite faith commitments enhance the dialogue and enlarge the possibilities of mutual efforts for the common good.

A Brilliant Pastoral Strategy

Contrary to Douthat's narrative, Francis has adopted a brilliant pastoral strategy that refuses to reduce morality to keeping rules and places this difficult issue in the framework of moving toward the high gospel ideal of one man and woman in a lifelong, faithful, mutually enriching, and socially beneficial relationship. By refusing to promulgate new rules, the pope encourages a more gospel-based morality that calls for prayerful discernment and fidelity to a properly formed conscience. This is not a weak compromise designed to keep from totally alienating liberals and conservatives. It is a Christ-like response by a wise pastor, who understands the dynamic interplay between gospel ideals and human limitations.

Francis's Response

For his part, Pope Francis, who does not mention his critics by name, distinguishes constructive criticisms guided by the Holy Spirit from those prompted by a "bad spirit" of triumphalism and "certain forms of strictness." He thinks that the critics of *Amoris Laetitia* do not understand the way the Holy Spirit has been guiding the Church since Vatican II. They see life in black-and-white terms, failing to appreciate the dynamic flow of life that calls for prayerful discernment of God's calling in individual circumstances. The pope notes that historians recognize that it takes a century to absorb the teachings of a Council, which means we are just at the halfway mark in appropriating the teachings of Vatican II. Concretely, Francis praised the document promulgated by the Argentine bishops, which essentially stated that priests in some exceptional cases could offer the help of the sacraments to divorced and remarried Catholics. This document, which endorses "a journey of discernment," offers, according to the pope, a proper interpretation of *Amoris Laetitia*.

We can imagine various positive responses to the pope's pastoral sensitivity. Some priests will find justification for their previous use of the internal forum; others will be more open to helping couples discern their position in the Church. Some divorced and remarried couples who now go to communion will be relieved of lingering guilt feelings and perhaps extend their involvement in the parish; others will be moved to talk to their pastors about participating in the sacraments. We all can learn important lessons from the pastoral wisdom of Pope Francis: maintain the high ideals of the gospel; avoid harsh judgments of others; prayerfully discern the next step forward on our spiritual journey; and have faith in the merciful God who calls us by name and never tires of forgiving.

6

CLERGY SEX-ABUSE ISSUES

When Jorge Bergoglio was elected Bishop of Rome in 2013, he inherited a horrendous, widespread clergy sex-abuse scandal. As we saw in chapter 1, both opponents and supporters of Francis were highly critical of his handling of the scandal during the first five years of his papacy. We can gain a better appreciation of the challenge presented to the new pope by recalling some of the history of clergy sex abuse in the Church.

HISTORY

Medieval Period

On the website of the Crusade Against Clergy Abuse, Thomas Doyle, a Dominican priest and a canon lawyer, argued that such abuse has been well documented throughout Church history. In 306, the Council of Elvira in Spain passed several canons imposing penalties on priests who committed adultery, fornication, and pederasty. Some of the *Penitential Books*, widely used from the sixth to the twelfth century in Ireland as a guide for confessors, advised severe penalties for clerics who commit sodomy with young boys. In the eleventh century, Cardinal Peter

Damian (1007–73), who lived in a society where clerical deca-
dence was generally accepted as almost normal, wrote the *Book
of Gomorrah*, demanding that superiors exclude sodomites from
ordination and dismiss from holy orders those who are given to
"unclean acts." Damian, declared a doctor of the Church in 1828,
showed special contempt for priests who defile boys who come to
them for confession. Very aware of the damage done by offending
clerics to their victims and to the Church, the reforming Benedictine saint appealed to Pope Leo IX with proposals to take decisive action. Unfortunately, the pope, who praised Damian for his
analysis, softened his proposals, while saying nothing about the
suffering of the victims.

In 1140, just a year after the Second Lateran Council first
mandated celibacy for all western clergy, the monk Gratian
published a collection of Church laws, commonly known as
"Gratian's Decree," which indicated, according to Doyle, that
adultery, casual sex, and homosexual relationships were rampant
among the clergy during the medieval period.

The Council of Trent

At the Council of Trent (1545–63), a significant minority
of bishops, who agreed with Luther and Calvin that mandatory
celibacy was not working, proposed a canon permitting priests
to be married. Rejecting this proposal, most bishops supported
a canon praising the state of virginity and reinforcing mandatory
celibacy. In the last of its twenty-five sessions, Trent dealt with
the problem of clergy concubinage, imposing penalties for guilty
priests and bishops. Reflecting on this history, Doyle noted that
"clergy sexual abuse of all kinds" was well known and continuous
despite a "constant stream" of ecclesial disciplinary legislation.
Church leaders made no attempt to hide the problem and, at
times, turned to secular authorities to impose punishments on
guilty clerics. Furthermore, some Church authorities recognized

that the problem was not only "dysfunctional clerics but irresponsible leadership."

The Contemporary Era

Moving into the contemporary era, Thomas Doyle highlighted the work of Father Gerald Fitzgerald (1884–1969), the founder of the Servants of the Paraclete, who established treatment centers for priests dealing with addiction issues. As early as 1952, he warned bishops that priests who have abused young boys could not be trusted to return to ministry and should be laicized. Fitzgerald, who was a spiritual director and not a psychologist, not only conveyed his view to some American bishops but also sent a written summary of his recommendations to the Vatican and met personally with the newly elected Pope Paul VI, arguing that incorrigible abusers of the young should be laicized. Unfortunately, Church leaders did not heed the warnings of Fitzgerald and others with disastrous results, including a mounting number of innocent victims and media headlines accusing bishops of reassigning abusive priests.

Lafayette, 1984

The first of those headlines appeared in 1984 in the celebrated case of Father Gilbert Gauthe of Lafayette, Louisiana, who later pled guilty to eleven counts of molestation of boys. In 1991, journalist Jason Berry, who covered the Gauthe case, published *Lead Us Not into Temptation: Catholic Priests and the Sexual Abuse of Children*, which brought to public attention the problem of abusive priests and the bishops who protected them. Court records, unsealed some three decades after the Gauthe trial, corroborated the fundamental charge that bishops moved accused priests from one parish to another without any notification or warning.

Boston, 2002

In early 2002, *The Boston Globe* published a series of articles on clergy sex abuse in the Boston archdiocese that led to the prosecution and conviction of five priests, including John Geoghan, who allegedly molested over 130 children. Under great pressure, Cardinal Bernard Law, who said he followed expert advice in reassigning accused priests, resigned as archbishop of Boston in December 2002, asking forgiveness for his "shortcomings and mistakes." Not only in Boston but all over the country long-silent victims courageously came forward with their stories of abuse. In this situation, the American bishops in June 2002 met in Dallas and approved the "Charter for the Protection of Children and Young People" that established a zero-tolerance policy for clergy sex abuse, including a pledge to provide a safe environment for youth participating in church activities and a requirement of background checks for church employees.

National Review Board

The American bishops also created a National Review Board, composed of bishops and respected Catholic laypersons, which commissioned the John Jay College of Criminal Justice to study the issue of clergy sexual abuse in U.S. dioceses from 1950 to 2002. The final John Jay Report, based on statistics supplied by dioceses, showed that 4.7 percent of the more than 100,000 priests and deacons ministering over a fifty-year period were accused of sexual abuse and 1 percent were convicted and imprisoned. The report found that 81 percent of victims were male, with most between the ages of eleven and seventeen. Almost 70 percent of the abusive priests were ordained before 1970, and about half were thirty-five years of age or younger when the first allegations occurred. On the practice of reassigning abusive priests, the report noted the typical defense was that bishops were following the best medical advice of the time, which indicated abusers could be rehabilitated and safely returned to ministry. Most reassigned priests received counseling, and about 40 percent went through treatment programs. The fact that some bishops failed to report allegations to law enforcement officials has led, according to the report, to state legislation requiring notification.

Settlements

By some estimates, the Catholic dioceses of the United States paid out more than $3 billion to settle claims of clergy sex abuse from 1950 to 2012. For example, the Diocese of Oregon settled nearly ninety cases for $100 million, and Boston made available $85 million for 552 alleged victims. At least eight dioceses declared bankruptcy due to sex-abuse cases, including Tucson and Davenport. Other dioceses settled cases out of court, reducing their resources available for pastoral and social services.

Annual Reports

Each year since 2002, the United States Conference of Catholic Bishops (USCCB) issues a report on implementing the Dallas Charter to extend compassionate care to victims, to report all abuse to authorities, to hold perpetrators accountable, and to continue efforts in education and prevention. For example, the 2013 report included the following facts: 936 allegations of abuse were made during the year, of which 136 were substantiated; 538 of the 730 accused were priests, 11 deacons, and 195 of unknown clerical status; 204 of the 730 were deceased; the alleged victims were mostly male (286 out of 365) with 40 percent between the ages of ten and fourteen. The report also indicated that the most frequent instances of abuse occurred in the 1970s, with a sharp decline in the decades since; between 2004 and 2013, the Church spent more than $2.7 billion in costs related to abuse allegations, including settlements and therapy for victims; finally, over 99 percent of priests have undergone background checks. This report appeared a few months after Francis was elected pope.

The 2018 report, issued just after five years of the Francis papacy, showed that 695 allegations nationwide were filed against priests, substantially down from the 2013 report. The audit, with its accompanying commentaries, noted, "While progress continues to be made, there are worrisome signs for the future," especially "a general complacency" evident in some unnamed dioceses. Some seem to think that clergy sex abuse is "an historic event of the past," ignoring the disturbing fact that the report found twenty-four allegations from current minors. One of the commentaries also noted the recent widespread publicity of sex-abuses cases, including the abuse of hundreds of female members of the U.S. gymnastics team. Recognizing this serious ongoing cultural problem, the report insisted, "The Church must more valiantly carry out Her pledge to prevent the abuse of children, and do more to support those who have been abused, whether within or outside of the Church."

Improving the Dallas Charter

Despite these efforts at transparency, critics in the United States contend that the Dallas Charter, which has been modified a couple of times in the past, needs improvements. For example, a watchdog group of priests, religious, and laypersons, known as the Catholic Whistleblowers, wrote a letter dated April 1, 2018, to Cardinal Daniel DiNardo, president of the USCCB, with a number of proposals, including extending the zero-tolerance policy for substantiated allegations to bishops complicit in abuse; posting on diocesan websites the names of abusers; and working with state legislatures to reform statutes of limitation laws. The group argues for these changes on the grounds that the sex-abuse scandal continues and "trust in the bishops remains damaged."

SOCIETAL, CULTURAL, AND ECCLESIAL FACTORS

Sadly, reports of clergy sex abuse have surfaced in countries all over the world. To take just one example, the Irish Catholic Church has been hit with a series of scandals involving thousands of victims, alleged cover-ups by four archbishops of Dublin, and charges that Cardinal Sean Brady participated in efforts to silence youthful victims. An insightful study, *Child Sex Abuse and the Catholic Church: Gender, Power, and Organizational Culture* (Oxford University Press, 2012), by University College Dublin lecturer Marie Keenan, emphasizes the societal, cultural, and ecclesial factors that have produced a pool of Irish priests prone to the sexual abuse of minors.

Seminary Training

Keenan, who studied both victims and perpetrators, argues that seminary training tends to turn out men who are underdeveloped emotionally and who find it difficult to establish healthy adult relationships. Celibacy is presented as a "gift," without attending to the "human-loss" it involves. In the practice of ministry, abusive priests were in a position of public power but often felt personally powerless. Operating out of a legalistic morality and negative notions of sexuality, they sought power and gratification in relationships with minors, considered as friends and not victims. The abusers studied by Keenan saw themselves first as priests called to live a life of perfect clerical celibacy and only secondly as men with normal sexual desires. They had few close relationships with other priests and no close adult relationships. Hard workers, they were outwardly subservient to Church authority but inwardly unhappy and discontented, a dangerous state that they tended to deny or ignore. For Keenan, the abusers do not fit the psychiatric classification of pedophilia. They are not flawed individuals with an overwhelming sexual drive. They get involved with minors, almost accidently in many cases, because all routes to healthy adult relationships seem closed to them as clergy.

The Cover-Up

The widespread cover-up in Ireland was facilitated, according to Keenan, by the great respect laypersons had for priests, based on their sacrifice of family life and their historical role in the struggle for national independence. People who revered their priests were not inclined to suspect any kind of danger for their children. The situation was exacerbated by the clerical culture, which failed to foster open conversation about sexual issues and was often devoid of honest interpersonal sharing. Some bishops moved perpetrators around, putting more emphasis on protecting the reputation of the institutional Church than protecting young persons. Civil authorities, immersed in the Irish culture of deference toward the Catholic Church, failed to respond adequately to the initial revelations of the clergy abuse of children.

Solutions

Keenan's work is extremely important since it reminds us that effective solutions cannot be confined to better policing of clergy and more accountability of bishops. We need improvement on fundamental issues, such as better seminary education, healthier attitudes toward sexuality, more realistic approaches to celibacy, more authentic relationships between clergy and laity, more fraternal relationships between bishops and priests, and more realistic expectations about the joys and sorrows of priestly ministry.

POPE JOHN PAUL II

Most of the media coverage of past cases of clergy sex abuse occurred during the long pontificate of Pope John Paul II (1978–2005), who took some positive steps to deal with the problem. In 2001, the pope sent an email to churches around the world apologizing for clergy sex abuse of children. In 2002, amid the Boston scandal, John Paul called the American cardinals to Rome for a discussion of the situation and issued a statement calling sex abuse "an appalling sin" and declaring the priesthood had no room for clergy abusers. He emphasized the need for better seminary training and condemned the arrogance of priests who lose their sense of service and become disheartened. John Paul also tried to educate curial leaders on the problem by sponsoring a three-day conference featuring presentations by psychiatrists on the causes of sexual abuse.

Cardinal Law

Critics of John Paul claim he mishandled some important cases. In 2004, he appointed Cardinal Bernard Law, who had resigned two years earlier as archbishop of Boston over his alleged cover-up of clergy sex-abuse cases, to the prestigious position of Archpriest of St. Mary Major in Rome. Catholics in the United States who knew that Law had reassigned abusive priests in Boston were outraged that he was honored in Rome. Furthermore, this appointment created problems for Pope Francis over funeral arrangements when Cardinal Law died in 2017.

In 1995, Cardinal Hans Hermann Groer, archbishop of Vienna, resigned over charges that he had sexual affairs with seminarians in the 1970s. Despite pleas from the Austrian bishops to Pope John Paul to denounce Groer, the pope continued to support him until he died in 2003, defending him against "unjust attacks" and calling him a "faithful servant."

The Maciel Case

The most telling criticism of John Paul concerns his relationship with the Mexican priest Marcial Maciel Degollado (1920–2008), who was the founder and director of the Legionaries of Christ from 1941 to 2006 and who was celebrated as a great fundraiser for the Church, a prolific recruiter of priests, and a founder of numerous schools and charitable institutes.

In 1998, a group of nine men lodged formal charges with the Vatican that Maciel had sexually abused them as young students. Despite these well-substantiated charges, the CDF under Cardinal Ratzinger did nothing, and John Paul continued to support Maciel, traveling with him on trips to Mexico and praising him for his work of recruiting priests. Only after Maciel's death in 2008 did it become public knowledge that he had fathered children by two different women, whom he supported financially, and had abused many other minors, including his own children. He died in St. Petersburg, Florida, without ever publicly admitting his guilt or asking forgiveness. Critics of John Paul use the Maciel case to argue that the pope did not really appreciate the gravity of the sex-abuse problem and did far too little to promote transparency and accountability.

POPE BENEDICT

In 2004, Cardinal Ratzinger, as head of the CDF, reopened the halted investigation of Father Maciel. After he was elected pope in 2005, Benedict removed Maciel from active ministry, imposing on him a "life of prayer and penance without any form of public ministry." Pope Benedict often held meetings with victims, some high profile, including a session with five persons abused in Boston, during which he expressed the concerns of the Church and asked for forgiveness. Later in his pontificate, the Centre for Child Protection (CCP), with ties to the Pontifical

Gregorian University in Rome, was established for the purpose of training pastoral caregivers to recognize and prevent child abuse. The CCP is a practical response to the strong sentiments of Benedict: "We must not tolerate the abuse of minors. We must defend minors and we must severely punish the abusers."

In 2010, Benedict initiated reforms in Maciel's Legionaries of Christ, which had instilled in their members a cult-like reverence for their founder. Soon afterward, leaders issued a statement about Maciel: "We accept and regret that given the gravity of his faults, we cannot take his person as a model of Christianity or priestly life." The statement left open many questions, including why leaders ignored incriminating evidence for so long, what to do about the cult of secrecy in the order, whether to use Maciel's writings in their seminaries, and how to handle new charges of abuse by Legionnaire priests.

Critics of Benedict

Critics of Pope Benedict contend that, while he served as archbishop of Munich in the 1980s, an abusive priest from Essen, Germany, was given therapy and assigned as a pastor in Munich, despite a warning of his psychiatrist that he should not be allowed to work with young children. He did abuse boys again and was convicted of a crime in 1986. The archdiocese has defended Benedict, insisting that the reassignment was handled by his vicar general, Gerhard Gruber, who has been reluctant to accept total responsibility.

Some advocates for abuse victims were critical of Benedict's meetings with victims, viewing them as cynical public relations gestures that fostered the illusion that real reform was forthcoming. Others argued that these meetings were acts of humility that serve as a model for Church leaders. There is general agreement that Benedict deserves higher marks for dealing with the scandal than does John Paul. Most commentators, however, believe that

Benedict did not do enough to hold complicit bishops account-able. They cite, for example, the case of Bishop Robert Finn of Kansas City, who was left in office by the pope even though he was legally convicted in 2012 of failing to inform the proper authorities about a suspected priest predator in his diocese. There remains a general sense in the secular world that, during the Benedict papacy, the Church was more concerned with protect-ing its reputation than protecting young persons and more reliant on secrecy than transparency.

POPE FRANCIS

This brief history reminds us that Pope Francis, elected in 2013, became the leader of a Church with a long history of clergy sexual misconduct, an unresolved abuse scandal, thousands of victims in need of help, millions of disillusioned Catholics, priests ill-equipped to deal with the pressures of pastoral ministry, bish-ops who avoided accountability for failed oversight, and recent popes who had made only limited progress in solving the crisis.

Commission for Protection of Minors

About a year after his election, Francis, already under attack for inaction, established the Pontifical Commission for the Pro-tection of Minors, with the task of proposing to the pope "the most opportune initiatives" to protect minors and vulnerable adults so that crimes of sexual abuse "are no longer repeated in the Church." Although the Commission, led by Cardinal Sean O'Malley, archbishop of Boston, worked with almost two hundred dioceses and religious communities worldwide to raise awareness of the problem of sex abuse, it has not really been an effective instrument for reform. The members soon realized that raising awareness was not enough and that the Church had to deal with complicit bishops who reassigned abusive priests. This led to the decision of Pope Francis to create a new tribunal to judge bishops accused of covering up for priest predators. Unfortunately, the Vatican bureaucracy was not able to solve many legal problems, and in 2016, Francis officially dropped the plan, leaving it to existing procedures to deal with complicit bishops.

Marie Collins

Of the seventeen members of the Commission, two were abuse survivors: Peter Saunders, who was ousted in 2016 for criticizing the Commission, and Marie Collins, a native of Ireland with experience as a victim and advocate. When Marie was thirteen, she was abused by a priest hospital chaplain while recovering from an operation. Feeling ashamed and guilty, she did not tell anyone while suffering from various debilitating emotional and physical ailments for over thirty years. When she was forty-seven, she told her doctor and her parish priest, who told her it was probably her fault, which set her back into another ten years of silent guilt and depression. In the 1990s, Collins, strengthened by growing news reports of clergy sex abuse, went to her archbishop who once again rebuffed her, advising her not to testify against her abuser in court. This time, Collins was so angry that she refused to remain silent and became an outspoken advocate for victims, especially by establishing the Marie Collins Foundation, which helps abused children.

After serving on the Pontifical Commission for three years, Collins resigned over its ineffectiveness. In an article published in the *National Catholic Reporter* in March 2017, she stated, "The most significant problem has been reluctance of some members of the Vatican Curia to implement the recommendations of the Commission despite their approval by the pope." Collins went on to list a number of specific stumbling blocks: lack of adequate funding during the first year; difficulties in communicating with various curial offices; the failure of the CDF to set up the Tribunal for bishops' accountability proposed by Francis; the reluctance of some in the Curia to cooperate with the Commission; and the "last straw" for Collins, the refusal of the Curia to implement the simple recommendation, approved by the pope, to ensure that all substantiated complaints from victims receive a response. While Collins, who felt a moral obligation to resign to retain her integrity, believes "the pope does at heart understand the horror of abuse and the need for those who would hurt minors to be stopped," she urged him to act by giving the Commission more power to oversee implementation of its recommendations. Marie Collins leaves us with the impression of a pope dedicated to dealing constructively and comprehensibly with the sex-abuse scandal but thwarted by an entrenched, self-serving Curia, which he has not been able to control.

Critics of Francis

Critics of Francis challenge this benign assessment in various ways: he did not have a scheduled meeting with victims when he visited the United States; he delayed establishing the Commission for a year after his election; he did not invest the necessary time or energy in gaining the cooperation of the Curia; he allowed the funeral of Cardinal Law to be held in St. Peter's Basilica; he did not meet personally with Marie Collins; and he let the Commission's three-year mandate expire in December 2017, while waiting until February 2018 to reestablish it.

CHILE

Supporters of Francis, as well as his opponents, severely criticized his initial response to the sex-abuse situation in Chile. Drawing on a timeline published by the Associated Press and other journalistic reports, we can recall some of the main events in the still-developing situation in Chile. In February 2011, a popular charismatic Chilean priest, Fernando Karadima, was convicted by the Vatican of abusing minors and forced out of ministry and into a life of prayer and penance away from minors. Karadima, who served in a very wealthy parish and had close ties to influential persons, was instrumental in promoting many vocations to the priesthood, some of whom became bishops. Those relationships proved to be crucial in subsequent developments in Chile, starting in 2015. On January 10 of that year, Francis appointed Juan Barros as bishop of Osorno over the objections of the Chilean bishops concerned about his complicity in the abuse committed by Karadima. On January 31, Francis wrote a letter acknowledging the concerns of the Chilean bishops but rejecting their plea to have Barros resign because, as the pope later said, there was no evidence of his involvement in a cover-up. In February, over a thousand Chilean Catholics in the Osorno diocese, lawmakers, priests, and laypersons, signed a petition urging Francis to revoke the Barros appointment. On March 21, Barros was installed as bishop of Osorno in a Mass marked by violent protests. On April 12, Juan Carlos Cruz wrote a letter accusing Barros of witnessing the sex abuse inflicted on him by Father Karadima, which was hand delivered from Marie Collins to Cardinal O'Malley, who personally gave it to Pope Francis. On May 15, Francis told a spokesperson for the Chilean bishops that the opposition to Barros comes from leftists who speak "nonsense" about him.

Chile in 2018

In the first part of 2018, events unfolded rapidly. On January 15, Pope Francis arrived in Chile, was greeted by unprecedented protests, apologized for the "irreparable damage" suffered by sex-abuse victims, and held two tearful meetings with survivors. On January 18, Francis responded to a journalist that there is "not one shred of proof" against Barros and that it is all calumny. On

January 20, Cardinal O'Malley publicly rebuked the pope, saying his comments about calumny "were a source of great pain" for abuse survivors. On January 21, while flying back to Rome, Francis repeated his charge of calumny, his claim that no victim has come forward with proof, and his conviction that Barros is innocent. On January 30, the Vatican appointed Archbishop Charles Scicluna to investigate the Chilean situation. On February 5, Cruz released his previous letter to the pope, decrying not only the abuse he suffered but also his subsequent "terrible mistreatment" by pastors. On February 17, Archbishop Scicluna met with Cruz for three hours in New York and then flew to Chile, where he took testimony from more than sixty witnesses. On March 21, fourteen priests were suspended in the diocese of Rancagoa for alleged abuse and sharing pornographic material. On April 11, Francis released a letter to the Chilean bishops admitting he made "serious errors in judgment," apologizing to victims, and inviting the victims to come to Rome so he could beg their forgiveness in person. On April 27, the pope began three days of meetings with Cruz and two other survivors, James Hamilton and Jose Murillo, who accepted the pope's apology and urged him to take concrete action to end the epidemic of abuse and cover-ups. From May 15–17, Francis spent three days in prayer and discussion with thirty-four Chilean bishops, who almost all submitted their resignation. From June 2–3, he met with more Chilean victims, including five priests. On June 11, the pope accepted three of the resignations, including that of Osorno Bishop Juan Barros, and appointed temporary leaders for each of those vacant dioceses. On June 12, Archbishop Scicluna and a colleague began a healing mission to Osorno. On June 28, the pope accepted two more resignations, including Bishop Goic, who courageously denounced human rights abuses under President Pinochet but admittedly failed to notify authorities of sexual abuse in his diocese.

Juan Cruz

We can get a better feel for the Chilean situation by viewing it from the perspective of one of the victims, Juan Carlos Cruz. Juan, the eldest of three sons of a well-to-do banker, was devasted when, as a fifteen-year-old, he had to deal with the sudden death of his father. Steeped in the Chilean Catholic culture, Juan sought help from his parish priest, Father Karadima, who took advantage of the distraught teenager and sexually abused him. This abusive relationship lasted about eight years until Juan, struggling to rise above his guilt and shame, completed a degree in journalism and took a job with a local television station. Still haunted by debilitating memories of his abuse, Juan emigrated to the United States in the early 2000s, settling in Philadelphia and working for Dupont as a communications and branding executive. In 2009, James Hamilton, another survivor of Karadima's abuse, contacted Cruz and gained his support in trying to bring to account not only Karadima but also priests and bishops who were complicit in his crimes. The courageous persistent effects of Cruz, Hamilton, and their fellow survivor Jose Murillo generally met resistance from the Chilean hierarchy but did contribute to the Vatican decision in 2011 to condemn Karadima for his multiple misdeeds and restrict him to a life of prayer and penance away from minors.

The Letter to Francis

When Cruz found out in January 2015 that Pope Francis had appointed Juan Barros as bishop for the small diocese of Osorno, he wrote to the pope an eight-page letter in Spanish dated March 3, 2015, describing his own abuse (forced kissing with the tongue, as he put it) by Karadima and insisting that Barros witnessed this on many occasions. In April 2015, after Barros was officially installed, Cruz gave his letter to Marie Collins who hand delivered it to Cardinal O'Malley (photos of this exchange are available), who later told both Collins and Cruz that he personally gave the letter to the pope. These details are important because Francis has consistently insisted that he had no direct knowledge of misdeeds by Barros.

At the beginning of his letter, Cruz told the pope that he was writing because he was "tired of fighting, crying, and suffering," so much so that "he wanted to kill himself." After suggesting many survivors were counting on Francis to listen to them, Cruz concluded with a personal note: "I treasure my faith, it's what sustains me, but it is slipping away from me."

When Francis visited Chile on January 7, 2018, he did meet with survivors and showed compassion, but he also repeated his charge that there was no evidence against Barros and that his opponents were "leftists" guilty of "calumny." Juan Cruz interpreted this statement as the pope calling him a liar, which hurt him deeply and prompted him to release to the press his original eight-page letter.

Meeting Scicluna

Soon after returning to Rome, Francis engaged Maltese Archbishop Charles Scicluna to do a thorough investigation of the situation in Chile. The archbishop began by meeting with Cruz for three hours in Holy Name Church in New York, after which Juan said that, for the first time in his long lonely journey, a Church official had actually heard him. After receiving the long scathing report from Scicluna, Francis apologized for misreading the situation and invited Cruz and his two colleagues to come to Rome so that he could personally ask for forgiveness.

Meeting Francis

During his conversation with Francis, Juan told the pope that a cardinal had chided him, suggesting he probably enjoyed the abuse because he was gay. In a widely quoted statement, Cruz said the pope responded, "God made you that way and loves you as you are" and added "the pope loves you as you are, you have to be happy with who you are."

After his private three-hour meeting with the pope in his residence, Cruz reported that they spoke in "great detail and pain" and it was "very raw." He said that he never saw "anyone so contrite" and quoted Francis as saying, "I was part of the problem and that's why I am saying sorry." Juan did not press Francis on whether he read his original letter describing the abuse but did say the pope was misinformed. Later, Cruz joined Hamilton and Murillo in saying they forgave the pope and in urging him to transform his "loving words into exemplary action." In their joint statement, they noted that for ten years they had been treated as enemies, but in their conversations with Francis, they "met the friendly face of the Church." Expressing his own sense of the great significance of the event, Cruz declared, "I feel like I was representing so many men and women of different ages, even some who have committed suicide, who are sick and tired of waiting, who walk around with this shame inside their bodies. We brought their pain with us. We want to make this the beginning of the end of this culture of abuse."

Later, when Cruz heard that Francis had fired Barros and sent Scicluna on a healing mission to Osorno, Cruz rejoiced: "A new day has begun in Chile's Catholic Church," adding that "the band of delinquent bishops" has begun "to disintegrate today." Looking ahead, he predicted that the "Chilean precedent will have a tsunami effect on what happens in other countries dealing with clergy-sex abuse."

Commentaries on Francis and Chile

Commenting on recent developments in Chile, *The Atlantic* ran an article, with an explicit reference to Juan Cruz, entitled

"The Pope's Turnaround in Sex Abuse May Have a Tsunami Effect" by Emma Green, who noted "an aggressive redirection" by Pope Francis and a "tonal change" from a defensive stand to a focus on "the pain of victims and the errors of the Church."

A *New York Times* editorial commented on the pope's apology: "Now, at long last, Pope Francis seems to have glimpsed the depths of the global crisis." Noting the great damage done to the Catholic Church worldwide by the clergy sex abuse, the editorial stated that Francis has made "a good and welcome start" by "opening his ears and heart to victims" but concluded that "this is just a start."

The *Guardian* published an editorial calling the developments in Chile "electrifying," noting that the pope told the Chilean bishops that the Scicluna report showed "a series of absolutely reprehensible acts…an unacceptable abuse of power, of conscience and sexual abuse." The editorial said the resignation of the Chilean bishops was a good thing but asked, "Will it be enough?" noting that Marie Collins thinks that resignation is too easy and there needs to be a proper disciplinary process as well.

Writing in *First Things* after the mass resignation of the Chilean bishops, Philip Lawler, author of *Lost Shepherd*, a very critical evaluation of the Francis papacy, claimed that Francis's response "will determine how history judges him." Lawler noted that the pope intervened unilaterally in Chile and did not use an established mechanism for disciplinary actions against offenders, suggesting that the Vatican does not have a working system in place for holding bishops accountable. The article brought up Chilean Cardinal Javier Errazuriz, a member of the Council of Cardinals, who has been accused of suppressing information about abuse. It also quoted a tweet by Marie Collins: "Chile: No resignation from Cardinal Errazuriz? No removal from the C9? No bishop removed—all allowed to resign. Really nothing changes." Lawler also accused Francis of lack of transparency for failing to disclose the process that led to the resignation of the Chilean bishops.

Positive Developments

Clearly, there are some positive developments coming out of the horrendous scandal in Chile. Pope Francis appears, now more than ever, as a human being who is willing to admit his mistakes and to seek forgiveness, as a Christian who has expanded his circle of compassion to include victims of abuse, and as the Bishop of Rome who holds bishops accountable. Survivors of clergy sex abuse around the world have new hope that their cries for help will eventually be heard. Potential priest abusers could possibly be deterred knowing that their misdeeds will not be routinely condoned by a secretive clerical culture. Complicit bishops cannot count on avoiding prosecution by civil and ecclesial authorities.

Remaining Questions

Nevertheless, serious questions remain as the Chilean story continues to unfold. Will Francis allow Cardinal Errazuriz to remain on the Council of Cardinals? Why did Francis not react immediately to the original letter from Juan Cruz? Will the pope accept more resignations of Chilean bishops? What institutional mechanisms will be put in place to resolve and heal the situation? Can Chile learn from the Dallas Charter and the constructive moves in the United States to protect minors? Will the Vatican establish a tribunal to try bishops accused of abuse and complicity? How will the experience in Chile effect the way clergy sex abuse is handled in other countries where we can expect more allegations to emerge?

More reports of clergy sex abuse continue to surface around the world in Europe, Asia, and Africa. The most striking case

comes from Australia, where Cardinal George Pell, a member of
the original Council of Cardinals established by Pope Francis,
was convicted in December 2018 of sexually abusing two young
boys while he was archbishop of Melbourne in the 1970s. Pell,
who has been removed from his position in the Council of Cardinals, has maintained his innocence and has filed an official
appeal.

THE PENNSYLVANIA REPORT

On August 14, 2018, the attorney general of Pennsylvania,
Josh Shapiro, released a report documenting the sexual abuse
of over one thousand children by some three hundred Catholic
priests over a seventy-year period in the Pennsylvania dioceses of
Allentown, Erie, Greensburg, Harrisburg, Pittsburgh, and Scran-
ton. The 1,356-page report, compiled by a grand jury that spent
more than two years investigating the abuse and the institutional
cover-up by Church leaders, summarized their findings: "Priests
were raping little boys and girls, and the men of God who were
responsible for them not only did nothing; they hid it all. For
decades."

The report, which contains lurid details, generated various public responses: empathy for deeply wounded survivors;
anger at priest predators and complicit bishops; distress over still
more scandals, including allegations against Cardinal Theodore
McCarrick, now restricted from public ministry; dissatisfac-
tion with the apologies of Church leaders who are still fighting
changes in the statute of limitations that protect abusive priests
from prosecution; and support for dedicated priests burdened by
the transgressions of their colleagues in ministry.

After a careful study of the Grand Jury Report, the respected
journalist Peter Steinfels, a former religion editor for the *New York
Times*, published a lengthy article in the January 9, 2019, issue of

Commonweal, arguing that the report's blanket condemnation of Church leaders for systematically covering up the crimes of abusive clergy and shielding the perpetrators is "grossly misleading, irresponsible, inaccurate, and unjust." Drawing on material in the report, Steinfels makes the case that the 2002 Dallas Charter has worked—though imperfectly—by improving the performance of bishops in protecting minors and removing abusive priests from ministry. The headline claim that the bishops did nothing while children were being raped is simply not true. Steinfels supports his case with a good deal of empirical evidence, aware that he is bucking a commonly accepted narrative and is subject to the charge that he is aiding the cover-up. He concludes his article with the suggestion that the American bishops have developed effective procedures for dealing with clergy sex abuse that can benefit other national hierarchies. The broad historical perspective developed by Steinfels will be a valuable resource as we try to make sense out of surely other forthcoming grand jury reports.

THE LETTER
TO THE PEOPLE OF GOD

On August 20, 2018, Pope Francis issued a two-thousand-word letter to the people of God, confessing "with shame and repentance," that "we did not act in a timely manner," especially given "the gravity of the damage done to so many lives." "We showed no care for the little ones; we abandoned them." The pope insisted that the Church must condemn "the atrocities perpetrated by consecrated persons" against "the most vulnerable," adding "let us beg forgiveness for our own sins and those of others." Francis is convinced that the whole people of God must be involved in developing effective solutions to the sex-abuse scandal. He is leery of solutions that come from the hierarchy and rely exclusively on implementation by the clergy.

Noting the worldwide efforts to find "necessary means" to protect children and vulnerable adults and to hold perpetrators accountable, the pope made this enigmatic statement: "We have delayed in applying these actions and sanctions that are so necessary, yet I am confident that they will help to guarantee a greater culture of care in the present and future." Although these "actions and sanctions" are unspecified, swift and decisive action is clearly needed as the scandals multiply.

Francis goes on to call for "a personal and communal conversion" that engages all God's people in creating a "culture of care" that says "never again" to every form of abuse and an emphatic no to all forms of "clericalism" that perpetuate the "culture of abuse." The pope encourages all of us to engage in penance and prayer, so we can work together in solidarity to eradicate this horrendous evil, each of us doing our part.

THE VIGANO STATEMENT

Shortly after the release of the papal letter, Archbishop Carlo Maria Vigano, Vatican nuncio to the United States from 2011 to 2016, issued an eleven-page statement accusing Pope Francis of lifting sanctions on Cardinal Theodore McCarrick previously imposed by Pope Benedict and of making McCarrick "his trusted counselor." Vigano, who was removed as nuncio by Francis, ended his statement with a call for the resignation of the pope and all involved in the cover-up, including Cardinal Donald Wuerl, who succeeded McCarrick as archbishop of Washington.

For his part, Pope Francis, who recently removed McCarrick from the College of Cardinals and from public ministry, has refused to comment on the Vigano statement, telling reporters, "I will not say a single word on this. I think this statement speaks for itself, and you have the sufficient journalistic capacity to draw conclusions."

The Vigano statement and the pope's silence have generated diverse reactions. *First Things* ran an article by Rev. Gerald Murray calling Vigano's confession an "eminently coherent account of his personal interactions with Francis." Castigating the pope for his silence, Murray asked, "How likely is it that an innocent man would let these multiple serious charges of malfeasance remain unanswered?" The article claims the pope's silence leaves people confused, distrustful, and ill-equipped to determine the truth of the claims. Murray ends his article by insisting that Francis tell "the Church what he knew and did regarding McCarrick."

George Weigel, who knew Vigano well during his years as nuncio, praised the archbishop as a "courageous reformer," an honest man, and a "loyal churchman," hoping that this testimony will "help others consider his very, very serious claims thoughtfully."

Atlantic journalist Emma Green noted that the Vigano letter has been a "major hit" to the credibility of Pope Francis. Acknowledging that the letter may be colored by "vicious hierarchy infighting," Green thinks it still exposes "the simmering discontent" of conservative clergy in Rome, the "vitriol surrounding the pope's handling of sex abuse," and the credibility problem he faces among the "faithful in the Church."

Jesuit author Thomas Reese published a column in the *National Catholic Reporter* noting Vigano's previous problems with Francis, who ignored his suggestions for new bishops and his questions about the orthodoxy of communion for the divorced. Interestingly, Vigano did not criticize Pope John Paul for appointing McCarrick as archbishop of Washington and as a member of the College of Cardinals, blaming instead his secretary of state Cardinal Angelo Sodano. Reese challenges Vigano's claim that Benedict sanctioned McCarrick sometime around 2009, pointing out that McCarrick continued performing public ministry to 2018 when Francis removed him. According to Reese, not only is there reason to doubt that Benedict sanctioned McCarrick, there is no evidence that Francis rescinded restrictions intended by Benedict. Furthermore, Vigano claims that he told Pope Francis on June 23, 2013, that McCarrick "corrupted generations of seminarians and priests" and that Benedict "ordered him to withdraw to a life of prayer and penance." Reese contends that Francis made a mistake in not immediately commenting on the alleged conversation and advises him to provide an honest clarification soon.

In an edited interview, theologian Massimo Faggioli claims Vigano, who opposes the efforts of the pope to welcome LGBT persons into the Church, is "using the right-wing rhetoric in the United States against Francis to rally ideological forces that are interested in regime change in the Catholic Church because they think Francis is a heretic." Faggioli also calls Vigano's claim that Benedict imposed canonical sanctions on McCarrick "absurd," since he continued to minister publicly. It is remarkable that Vigano says nothing about John Paul, who appointed McCarrick, but accuses Francis, the only one who "took visible measures against McCarrick." Faggioli does think Francis has been "excruciatingly slow" in dealing with the sex-abuse crisis but points out that he did fire McCarrick and other bishops, something his papal predecessors failed to do. He believes the pope made a good decision not to address the Vigano statement during his in-flight press conference returning from Ireland but that he must do so at some point for the good of the Church.

In Defense of Pope Francis

Despite the pressure to defend himself, Francis has chosen not to reply directly to the charges of Archbishop Vigano. However, the prefect for the Congregation for Bishops, Cardinal Marc Ouellet, has come to the pope's defense with a scathing personal letter to Vigano on October 7, 2018, calling his published accusations against the pope "incredible and far-fetched," "abhorrent" and politically motivated to hurt Francis. Ouellet denied that there were sanctions formally imposed by Pope Benedict on Cardinal McCarrick that were then invalidated by Pope Francis. He pointed out that Francis had nothing to do with McCarrick's promotions to bishop, archbishop, and cardinal, and that he stripped him from his cardinal's dignity as soon as there were credible accusations of abuse of a minor. Praising Francis for his pastoral sensitivity, Ouellet urged Vigano to repent and "come back to better feelings toward the Holy Father."

THE UNITED STATES

Here, in the United States, we can anticipate further developments regarding clergy sex abuse. More states will hold grand jury investigations and will eventually make public their findings, keeping the issue alive for years to come. As the discussion continues, it will become clear that the problem has institutional roots and requires systemic changes. We cannot solve the real problem simply by better policing of clergy and more accountability of bishops. The Church needs better seminary formation that will help candidates achieve a more mature psychosexual development. Making celibacy optional would increase the pool of candidates, allow for higher admission standards, and enrich the clerical ranks. Taking classes at universities with excellent theology departments would get seminarians out of a restricted all-male environment and provide them with a broader educational experience. Including more female professors and spiritual directors in seminaries would enrich formation programs. Men taking on the responsibility of a celibate lifestyle need a realistic understanding of the challenges and the personal diminishments that naturally occur without a spouse. Celibate clergy do not have a legitimate sex partner or a spouse to offer loving criticisms or a companion readily available for comfort and conversation.

Celibates do not have to learn how to manage the daily demands of making an intimate relationship work.

It is crucial to examine the existing clerical culture to identify the dynamics that enable clergy abuse and foster cover-ups. Priests need colleagues open to honest conversation about sexuality and the challenges of celibacy. Bringing more honest sharing into the clerical culture is complicated by the fact that many gay priests are reluctant to disclose their sexual orientation, understandably so since the Church officially deems it a disordered condition. Celibate clergy need healthy adult relationships with both men and women—something generally lacking in the lives of abusive clergy.

There is consensus that Pope Francis must show decisive leadership. He needs to make a credible response to Vigano and to implement his promised institutional reforms, including the creation of a Vatican tribunal to try complicit bishops.

In 2018, over three thousand Catholic theologians, educators, and lay leaders signed a statement that includes this proposal: "Today we call on the Catholic Bishops of the United States to prayerfully and genuinely consider submitting to Pope Francis their collective resignation as a public act of repentance and lamentation before God and God's People." Theologians who signed felt a need for dramatic action that would demonstrate the gravity of the problem and the need for constructive solutions. My own sense is that we can make more real progress by encouraging our current reform-minded bishops to support the radical changes needed to manage better this scandalous problem.

We should not forget the progress made by the provisions of the 2002 Dallas Charter in reducing the number of new substantiated allegations of abuse. The Charter, which does need improvements, can still serve as a model for other countries as they confront their own scandals.

We can hope that Pope Francis will find creative ways of mobilizing the entire Catholic community to extend better care to victims, to build on the progress already made in reducing the incidents of abuse, and to begin the radical work of improving seminary education, developing more realistic approaches to celibacy, and bringing greater openness and honesty into the clerical culture.

THE VATICAN SUMMIT

Francis tried to seize the initiative by calling Church leaders from around the world to a major meeting in Rome from February 21 to 24, 2019, on "protection of minors in the church." One of the members of the steering committee, Archbishop Charles Scicluna, who played an important role in dealing with the crisis in Chile, gave an interview to *America* magazine clarifying the purpose and dynamics of the meeting. Participants included the presidents of over one hundred bishops' conferences, the leaders of Eastern-Rite Catholic Churches, curial prefects, major superiors of religious orders, and representatives of abuse victims. The meeting consisted of plenary sessions, language-group discussions, listening sessions, prayer times, and a penitential liturgy. Scicluna emphasized that Francis realizes that clergy sex abuse is a "global issue" that "has to be top on the church's agenda." The Church needs to approach this crucial issue with a united front, with a firm resolve, and with respect for diverse cultures. Scicluna stated that the Vatican meeting is "not going to solve everything," but it is an important start of a synodal process involving all the members of the Church in communities around the world. The pope urged the bishops at the meeting "to listen to victims, to talk to experts and to listen to each other" so that they are able to carry out a "synodal approach" back home, which means utilizing the expertise and gifts of the laity in a collaborative effort to safeguard young persons and prevent abuse "in every parish, in every school, in every diocese."

As the Scicluna interview suggests, the key to understanding the strategy of Francis in calling the summit is his commitment to "synodality," his conviction that top-down solutions are ineffective, his belief that wisdom resides in the people of God, his trust in honest dialogue and mutual collaboration, and his hope that the local churches, guided by the Holy Spirit, will implement the new universal laws designed to deal with the horrendous worldwide scandal more openly, rapidly, and effectively.

Epilogue

A SYNODAL CHURCH

I hope that this book will serve several constructive functions: provide a balanced reading of the Francis papacy that challenges the predominantly negative evaluations by influential conservative critics; clarify the pope's positions in the context of significant historical and theological perspectives; highlight his pastoral approach to specific issues that transcends the political concerns of his critics; reveal aspects of his thought and practice easily missed by thematic summaries of his policies and accomplishments; and acknowledge the limitations and failures of the still-evolving Francis papacy as it strives to become more effective in its ministry.

In his commitment to ecclesial renewal, Francis puts great emphasis on what he calls a "synodal Church," as we saw at the end of the last chapter. In an address commemorating the fiftieth anniversary of the institution of the Synod of Bishops, the pope noted that the contemporary world demands a Church committed to "journeying together," as the word *synod* suggests. "Synodality is a constitutive element of the Church," which is "the most appropriate interpretative framework" for understanding its ministry and mission. This requires "mutual listening" so that all the members of the Church are heard and can function as both teachers and learners, while listening to the Holy Spirit together.

In a synodal Church, "there is a dynamism of communion which inspires all ecclesial decisions."

At the parish level, leaders and organizations "keep connected to the base" and are responsive to "people and their daily problems." At the universal level, Francis favors a "sound decentralization," based on his conviction that the pope should not "take the place of local bishops in the discernment of every issue which arises in their territory." In a synodal Church, the laity, the bishops, and the pope work together, "all listening to each other, and all listening to the Holy Spirit," in order to "bring about a more beautiful and humane world for coming generations."

For Pope Francis, synodality is the key to making progress on all our complex problems: listening to the voices of women seeking greater roles in the Church; listening to the moral demands of the gospel for a more just economic order; listening to the Vatican II program for liturgical renewal; and listening to the Spirit as the divorced and remarried make decisions about receiving communion. As to the vexing issue of clergy sex abuse, there will be no simple, easy, acceptable, complete, definitive solutions. The synodal strategy of Francis, however, offers the best opportunity to make meaningful progress at the local level, where the whole community can work together to protect children, assist survivors, and remove perpetrators. We can all hope that this strategy of Francis, the first Jesuit and Latin American Bishop of Rome, will indeed help the Church be a more credible sign and effective instrument of God's reign in today's world.